SCIENTIFIC
AMERICAN™
CUTTING-EDGE SCIENCE™

# The Nanotech
# Revolution

New York

Published in 2007 by The Rosen Publishing Group, Inc.
29 East 21st Street, New York, NY 10010

The articles in this book first appeared in the pages of *Scientific American*,
as follows: "Plenty of Room, Indeed" by Michael Roukes, September 2001;
"The Nanodrive Project" by Peter Vettiger and Gerd Binnig, January 2003;
"Innovations: Nano Patterning" by Gary Stix, March 2004; "The First
Nanochips" by G. Dan Hutcheson, April 2004; "Nanotechnology and the
Double Helix" by Nadrian C. Seeman, June 2004; "Nanotubes in the Clean
Room" by Gary Stix, February 2005; "Crossbar Nanocomputers" by Philip
J. Kuekes, Gregory S. Snider, and R. Stanley Williams, November 2005.

First Edition

**Library of Congress Cataloging-in-Publication Data**

The nanotech revolution.—1st ed.
    p. cm.—(Scientific American cutting-edge science)
Includes bibliographical references and index.
ISBN-13: 978-1-4042-0990-9
ISBN-10: 1-4042-0990-5 (library binding)
1. Nanotechnology—Popular works. I. Scientific American.
T174.7.N366 2007
620'.5—dc22

2006024270

*Manufactured in the United States of America*

**On the cover:** Microscopic nanobots work on human blood cells.
Background image: Arrays of cantilever-mounted tips inscribe millions
of digital bits on a plastic surface in an exceedingly small space.

**Illustration credits:** Cover (foreground nanobots) Michael Knight; cover
background, pp. 34, 35, 36, 63, 65, 67, 70, 73 Bryan Christie Design; p. 20
Nina Finkel; p. 24 Bryan Christie; p. 29 Slim Films; pp. 50, 52 Samuel
Velasco; p. 57 Lucy Reading/Sources: Intel and International Technology
Roadmap for Semiconductors; pp. 78, 82, 90 (right) Ken Eward BioGrafx;
pp. 84, 90 (left), 92, 93 (center) Alice Y. Chen; p. 87 Jen Christiansen;
p. 93 (top, bottom) Nadrian C. Seeman; pp. 106, 109, 110 Jean Francois
Povedin; p. 121 Slim Films/Source: Warren Robinett.

# Contents

# Introduction

Good things come in small packages. That, surely, is the mantra of today's researchers working in the nascent field of nanotechnology. What on earth is nanotech, you ask? Well, simply put, it's the science of the small. And chances are, if it hasn't already found its way into your life, it will in the not-so-distant future.

In this compilation of articles published over the past five years, leading authorities trace the steps scientists have taken in ushering us into the nano age—and make predictions about what is to come. Michael Roukes describes the unique mesoscale realm in which nanotechnological devices exist and contends that engineers will not be able to make reliable nanodevices until they understand the physical principles that govern matter there. Peter Vettiger and Gerd Binnig recount their efforts to build the first "nanodrive"—a micromechanical digital storage device with nano-size components. And Nadrian C. Seeman explains how DNA is an ideal molecule for building nano-scale structures that hold molecule-size electronic devices, or guest molecules for crystallography.

Other articles examine the promise of carbon nanotubes, the prospects for self-assembling nanostructures and ways to circumvent the problems inherent in the nanowires that will form the basis for tomorrow's nanocomputing circuitry. —**The Editors**

# I. "Plenty of Room, Indeed"

by Michael Roukes

*There is plenty of room for practical innovation at the nanoscale. But first, scientists have to understand the unique physics that governs matter there*

Back in December 1959, future Nobel laureate Richard Feynman gave a visionary and now oft-quoted talk entitled "There's Plenty of Room at the Bottom." The occasion was an American Physical Society meeting at the California Institute of Technology, Feynman's intellectual home then and mine today. Although he didn't intend it, Feynman's 7,000 words were a defining moment in nanotechnology, long before anything "nano" appeared on the horizon.

> *"What I want to talk about,"* he said, *"is the problem of manipulating and controlling things on a small scale. . . . What I have demonstrated is that there is room—that you can decrease the size of things in a practical way. I now want to show that there is plenty of room. I will not now discuss how we are going to do it, but only what is possible in principle. . . . We are not doing it simply because we haven't yet gotten around to it."*

The breadth of Feynman's vision is staggering. In that lecture 42 years ago he anticipated a spectrum of scientific and technical fields that are now well established, among them electron-beam and ion-beam fabrication, molecular-beam epitaxy, nanoimprint lithography, projection electron microscopy, atom-by-atom manipulation, quantum-effect electronics, spin electronics (also called spintronics) and micro-electromechanical systems (MEMS). The lecture also projected what has been called the "magic" Feynman brought to everything he turned his singular intellect toward. Indeed, it has profoundly inspired my two decades of research on physics at the nanoscale.

Today there is a nanotechnology gold rush. Nearly every major funding agency for science and engineering has announced its own thrust into the field. Scores of researchers and institutions are scrambling for a piece of the action. But in all honesty, I think we have to admit that much of what invokes the hallowed prefix "nano" falls a bit short of Feynman's mark.

We've only just begun to take the first steps toward his grand vision of assembling complex machines and circuits atom by atom. What can be done now is extremely rudimentary. We're certainly nowhere near being able to commercially mass-produce nanosystems—integrated multicomponent nanodevices that have the complexity and range of functions readily provided by modern microchips. But there is a fundamental science issue here as well. It is becoming increasingly clear that we are only *beginning* to acquire the detailed knowledge that will be at the heart of future nanotechnology. This new science concerns the properties and behavior of aggregates of atoms and molecules, at a scale not yet large enough to be considered macroscopic but far beyond what can be called microscopic. It is the science of the *mesoscale*, and until we understand it, practical devices will be difficult to realize.

Scientists and engineers readily fashion nanostructures on a scale of one to a few hundred nanometers—small indeed, but much bigger than simple molecules. Matter at this mesoscale is often awkward to explore. It contains too many atoms to be easily understood by straightforward application of quantum mechanics (although the fundamental laws still apply). Yet these systems are not so large as to be completely free of quantum effects; thus, they do not simply obey the classical physics governing the macroworld. It is precisely in this intermediate domain, the mesoworld, that unforeseen properties of collective systems emerge.

Researchers are approaching this transitional frontier using complementary top-down and bottom-up fabrication methods. Advances in top-down nanofabrication techniques such as electron-beam lithography (used extensively by my own research group) yield almost atomic-scale precision, but achieving success, not to mention reproducibility, as we scale down to the single-digit-nanometer regime becomes problematic. Alternatively, scientists are using bottom-up techniques for *self-assembly* of atoms. But the advent of preprogrammed self-assembly of arbitrarily large systems—with complexity comparable to that built every day in microelectronics, in MEMS and (of course) by Mother Nature—is nowhere on the horizon. It appears that the top-down approach will most likely remain the method of choice for building really complex devices for a good while.

Our difficulty in approaching the mesoscale from above or below bespeaks a basic challenge of physics. Lately, the essence of Feynman's "Plenty of Room" talk seems to be taken as a license for laissez-faire in nanotechnology. Yet Feynman never asserted that "anything goes" at the nanoscale. He warned, for instance, that the very act of trying to *"arrange the atoms one by one the way we want them"* is subject to fundamental principles: *"You can't put them so that they are chemically unstable, for example."*

Accordingly, today's scanning probe microscopes can move atoms from place to place on a prepared surface, but this ability does not immediately confer the power to build complex molecular assemblies at will. What has been accomplished so far, though impressive, is still quite limited. We will ultimately develop operational procedures to help us coax the formation of individual atomic bonds under more general conditions. But as we try to assemble complex networks of these bonds, they certainly will affect one another in ways we do not yet understand and, hence, cannot yet control.

Feynman's original vision was clearly intended to be inspirational. Were he observing now, he would surely be alarmed when people take his projections as some sort of gospel. He delivered his musings with characteristic playfulness as well as deep insight. Sadly for us, the field that would be called nanotechnology was just one of many that intrigued him. He never really continued with it, returning to give but one redux of his original lecture, at the Jet Propulsion Laboratory in 1983.

## New Laws Prevail

In 1959, and even in 1983, the complete physical picture of the nanoscale was far from clear. The good news for researchers is that, by and large, it still is! Much exotic territory awaits exploration. As we delve into it, we will uncover a panoply of phenomena that we must understand before practical nanotechnology will become possible. The past two decades have seen the elucidation of entirely new, fundamental physical principles that govern behavior at the mesoscale. Let's consider three important examples.

In the fall of 1987 graduate student Bart J. van Wees of the Delft University of Technology and Henk van Houten of the Philips Research Laboratories (both in the Netherlands) and their collaborators were studying the flow of electric current through what are now called quantum-point contacts. These are narrow conducting paths within a semiconductor, along which electrons are forced to flow [*see illustration on page 20*]. Late one evening van Wees's undergraduate assistant, Leo Kouwenhoven, was measuring the conductance through the constriction as he varied its width systematically. The research team was expecting to see only subtle conductance effects against an otherwise smooth and unremarkable background response. Instead there appeared a very pronounced, and now characteristic, staircase pattern. Further analysis that night revealed that plateaus were occurring at regular, precise intervals.

David Wharam and Michael Pepper of the University of Cambridge observed similar results. The two discoveries represented the first robust demonstrations of the *quantization of electrical conductance.* This is a basic property of small conductors that occurs when the wavelike properties of electrons are coherently maintained from the "source" to the "drain"—the input to the output—of a nanoelectronic device.

Feynman anticipated, in part, such odd behavior: "*I have thought about some of the problems of building electric circuits on a small scale, and the problem of resistance is serious. . . .*" But the experimental discoveries pointed out something truly new and fundamental: quantum mechanics can completely govern the behavior of small electrical devices.

Direct manifestations of quantum mechanics in such devices were envisioned back in 1957 by Rolf Landauer, a theoretician at IBM who pioneered ideas in nanoscale electronics and in the physics of computation. But only in the mid-1980s did control over materials and nanofabrication begin to provide access to this regime in the laboratory. The 1987 discoveries heralded the heyday of "mesoscopia."

A second significant example of newly uncovered mesoscale laws that have led to nascent nanotechnology was first postulated in 1985 by Konstantin Likharev, a young physics professor at Moscow State University working with postdoctoral student Alexander Zorin and undergraduate Dmitri Averin. They anticipated that scientists would be able to control the movement of single electrons on and off a "coulomb island," a conductor weakly coupled to the rest of a nanocircuit. This could form the basis for an entirely new type of device, called a single-electron transistor. The physical effects that arise when putting a single electron on a coulomb island become increasingly robust as the island is scaled downward. In very small devices, these single-electron charging effects can completely dominate the current flow.

Such considerations are becoming increasingly important technologically. Projections from the International Technology Roadmap for Semiconductors, prepared by long-range thinkers in the industry, indicate that by 2014 the minimum feature size for transistors in computer chips will decrease to 20 nanometers. At this dimension, each switching event will involve the equivalent of only about eight electrons. Designs that properly account for single-electron charging will become crucial.

By 1987 advances in nanofabrication allowed Theodore A. Fulton and Gerald J. Dolan of Bell Laboratories to construct the first single-electron transistor [*see illustration on page 24*]. The single-electron charging they observed, now called the coulomb blockade, has since been seen in a wide array of structures. As experimental devices get smaller, the coulomb blockade phenomenon is becoming the rule, rather than the exception, in weakly coupled nanoscale devices. This is especially true in experiments in which electric currents are

## Overview/Nanophysics

- Smaller than macroscopic objects but larger than molecules, nanotechnological devices exist in a unique realm—the mesoscale—where the properties of matter are governed by a complex and rich combination of classical physics and quantum mechanics.
- Engineers will not be able to make reliable or optimal nanodevices until they comprehend the physical principles that prevail at the mesoscale.
- Scientists are discovering mesoscale laws by fashioning unusual, complex systems of atoms and measuring their intriguing behavior.
- Once we understand the science underlying nanotechnology, we can fully realize the prescient vision of Richard Feynman: that nature has left plenty of room in the nanoworld to create practical devices that can help humankind.

passed through individual molecules. These molecules can act like coulomb islands by virtue of their weak coupling to electrodes leading back to the macroworld. Using this effect to advantage and obtaining robust, reproducible coupling to small molecules (in ways that can actually be engineered) are among the important challenges in the new field of molecular electronics.

In 1990, against this backdrop, I was at Bell Communications Research studying electron transport in mesoscopic semiconductors. In a side project, my colleagues Larry Schiavone and Axel Scherer and I began developing techniques that we hoped would elucidate the quantum nature of *heat* flow. The work required much more sophisticated nanostructures than the planar devices used to investigate mesoscopic electronics. We needed freely suspended devices, structures possessing full three-dimensional relief. Ignorance was bliss; I had no idea the experiments would be so involved that they would take almost a decade to realize.

The first big strides were made after I moved to Caltech in 1992, in a collaboration with John M. Worlock of the University of Utah and two successive postdocs in my group. Thomas S. Tighe developed the methods and devices that generated the first direct measurements of heat flow in nanostructures. Subsequently, Keith C. Schwab revised the design of the suspended nanostructures and put in place ultrasensitive superconducting instrumentation to interrogate them at ultralow temperatures, at which the effects could be seen most clearly.

In the late summer of 1999 Schwab finally began observing heat flow through silicon nitride nano-bridges. Even in these first data the fundamental limit to heat flow in mesoscopic structures emerged. The manifestation of this limit is now called the thermal conductance quantum. It determines the maximum rate at which heat can be carried by an individual wavelike mechanical vibration, spanning from the input to the output of a nanodevice. It is analogous to the electrical conductance quantum but governs the transport of heat.

This quantum is a significant parameter for nano-electronics; it represents the ultimate limit for the power-dissipation problem. In brief, all "active" devices require a little energy to operate, and for them to operate stably without overheating, we must design a way to extract the heat they dissipate. As engineers try to ever increase the density of transistors and the clock rates (frequencies) of microprocessors, the problem of keeping microchips cool to avoid complete system failure is becoming monumental. This will only become further exacerbated in nano-technology.

Considering even this complexity, Feynman said, *"Let the bearings run dry; they won't run hot because the heat escapes away from such a small device very, very rapidly."* But our experiments indicate that nature is a little more restrictive. The thermal conductance quantum can place limits on how effectively a very small device can dissipate heat. What Feynman envisioned can be correct only if the nanoengineer designs a structure so as to take these limits into account.

From the three examples above, we can arrive at just one conclusion: we are only starting to unveil the complex and wonderfully different ways that nanoscale systems behave. The discovery of the electrical and thermal conductance quanta and the observation of the coulomb blockade are true discontinuities—abrupt changes in our understanding. Today we are not accustomed to calling our discoveries "laws." Yet I have no doubt that electrical and thermal conductance quantization and single-electron-charging phenomena are indeed among the universal rules of nanodesign. They are new laws of the nanoworld. They do not contravene but augment and clarify some of Feynman's original vision. Indeed, he seemed to have anticipated their emergence: *At the atomic level, we have new kinds of forces and new kinds of possibilities, new kinds of effects. The problems of manufacture and reproduction of materials will be quite different.*

We will encounter many more such discontinuities on the path to true nanotechnology. These welcome windfalls will occur in direct synchrony with advances in our ability to observe, probe and control nanoscale structures. It would seem wise, therefore, to be rather modest and circumspect about forecasting nanotechnology.

# The Boon and Bane of Nano

The nanoworld is often portrayed by novelists, futurists and the popular press as a place of infinite possibilities. But as you've been reading, this domain is not some ultraminiature version of the Wild West. *Not* everything goes down there; there are *laws*. Two concrete illustrations come from the field of nano-electromechanical systems (NEMS), in which I am currently active.

Part of my research is directed toward harnessing small mechanical devices for sensing applications. Nanoscale structures appear to offer revolutionary potential; the smaller a device, the more susceptible its physical properties to alteration. One example is resonant detectors, which are frequently used for sensing mass. The vibrations of a tiny mechanical element, such as a small cantilever, are intimately linked to the element's mass, so the addition of a minute amount of foreign material (the "sample" being weighed) will shift the resonant frequency. Recent work in my lab by postdoc Kamil Ekinci shows that nanoscale devices can be made so sensitive that "weighing" individual atoms and molecules becomes feasible.

But there is a dark side. Gaseous atoms and molecules constantly adsorb and desorb from a device's surfaces. If the device is macroscopic, the resulting fractional change in its mass is negligible. But the change can be significant for nanoscale structures.

Gases impinging on a resonant detector can change the resonant frequency randomly. Apparently, the smaller the device, the less stable it will be. This instability may pose a real disadvantage for various types of futuristic electromechanical signal-processing applications. Scientists might be able to work around the problem by, for example, using arrays of nano-mechanical devices to average out fluctuations. But for individual elements, the problem seems inescapable.

A second example of how "not everything goes" in the nanoworld relates more to economics. It arises from the intrinsically ultralow power levels at which nanomechanical devices operate. Physics sets a funda-mental threshold for the minimum operating power: the ubiquitous, random thermal vibrations of a mechanical device impose a "noise floor" below which real signals become increasingly hard to discern. In practical use, nanomechanical devices are optimally excited by signal levels 1,000-fold or a millionfold greater than this threshold. But such levels are still a millionth to a billionth the amount of power used for conventional transistors.

The advantage, in some future nanomechanical signal-processing system or computer, is that even a million nanomechanical elements would dissipate only a millionth of a watt, on average. Such ultralow power systems could lead to wide proliferation and distribution of cheap, ultraminiature "smart" sensors that could continuously monitor *all* of the important functions in hospitals, in manufacturing plants, on aircraft, and so on. The idea of ultraminiature devices that drain their batteries extremely slowly, especially ones with sufficient computational power to function autonomously, has great appeal.

But here, too, there is a dark side. The regime of ultralow power is quite foreign to present-day electronics. Nanoscale devices will require entirely new system architectures that are compatible with amazingly low power thresholds. This prospect is not likely to be received happily by the computer industry, with its overwhelming investment in current devices and methodology. A new semiconductor processing plant today costs more than $1 billion, and it would probably have to be retooled to be useful. But I am certain that the revolutionary prospects of nanoscale devices will eventually compel such changes.

## Monumental Challenges

Certainly a host of looming issues will have to be addressed before we can realize the potential of nanoscale devices. Although each research area has its own concerns, some general themes emerge. Two challenges fundamental to my current work on nanomechanical systems, for instance, are relevant to nanotechnology in general.

*Challenge I: Communication between the macroworld and the nanoworld.* NEMS are incredibly small, yet their motion can be far smaller. For example, a nanoscale beam clamped on both ends vibrates

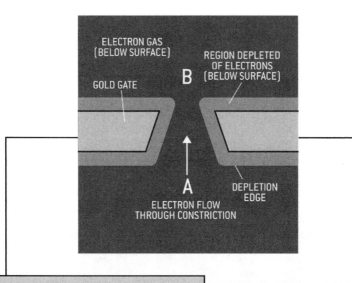

ELECTRON GAS
(BELOW SURFACE)

REGION DEPLETED
OF ELECTRONS
(BELOW SURFACE)

B

GOLD GATE

A

DEPLETION
EDGE

ELECTRON FLOW
THROUGH CONSTRICTION

One Step at a time

## QUANTIZATION OF ELECTRICAL CONDUCTANCE

In 1987 Bart J. van Wees and his collaborators at the Delft University of Technology and Philips Research Laboratories (both in the Netherlands) built a novel structure that revealed a basic law governing nanotech circuits. Gold gate electrodes were placed atop a semiconductor substrate. Within the substrate, a planar sheet of charge carriers, called a two-dimensional electron gas, was created about 100 nanometers below the surface. The gates and the gas acted like the plates of a capacitor.

When a negative voltage bias was applied to the gates, electrons within the gas underneath the gates, and slightly beyond the gates' periphery, were pushed away. (The diagram shows this state.) When increasing negative voltage was applied, this "depletion edge" became more pronounced. At a certain threshold, carriers on either side of the constriction (*between points A and B*) became separated, and the conductance through the device was zero. From this threshold level, conductance did not resume smoothly. Instead it increased in stepwise fashion, where the steps occurred at values determined by twice the charge of the electron squared, divided by Planck's constant. This ratio is now called the electrical conductance quantum, and it indicates that electric current flows in nanocircuits at rates that are quantized.

with minimal harmonic distortion when its vibration amplitude is kept below a small fraction of its thickness. For a 10-nanometer-thick beam, this amplitude is only a few nanometers. Building the requisite, highly efficient transducers to transfer information from such a device to the macroworld involves reading out information with even greater precision.

Compounding this problem, the natural frequency of the vibration increases as the size of the beam is decreased. So to usefully track the device's vibrations usefully, the ideal NEMS transducer must be capable of resolving extremely small displacements, in the picometer-to-femtometer (trillionth to quadrillionth of a meter) range, across very large bandwidths (extending into the microwave range). These twin requirements pose a truly monumental challenge, one much more significant than those faced so far in MEMS work. A further complication is that most of the methodologies from MEMS are inapplicable; they simply do not scale down well to nanometer dimensions.

These difficulties in communication between the nanoworld and the macroworld represent a generic issue in the development of nanotechnology. Ultimately, the technology will depend on robust, well-engineered information transfer pathways from what are, in essence, individual macromolecules. Although the grand vision of futurists may involve self-programmed nanobots that need direction from the macroworld only when they are first wound up and set in motion, it seems more likely that most nanotechnological applications realizable in our lifetimes will entail some form of reporting up to the macroworld and feedback and control back down. The communication problem will remain central.

Orchestrating such communication immediately invokes the very real possibility of collateral damage. Quantum theory tells us that the process of measuring a quantum system nearly always perturbs it. This can hold true even when we scale up from atoms and molecules to nanosystems comprising millions or billions of atoms. Coupling a nanosystem to probes that report back to the macroworld always changes the nanosystem's properties to some degree, rendering it less than ideal. Introducing the transducers required for communication will do more than just increase the nanosystem's size and complexity. They will also necessarily extract some energy to perform their measurements and can degrade the nanosystem's performance. Measurement always has its price.

*Challenge II: Surfaces.* As we shrink MEMS to NEMS, device physics becomes increasingly dominated by the surfaces. Much of the foundation of solid-state physics rests on the premise that the surface-to-volume ratio of objects is infinitesimal, meaning that physical properties are always dominated by the physics of the bulk. Nanoscale systems are so small that this assumption breaks down completely.

For example, mechanical devices patterned from single-crystal, ultrapure materials can contain very few (even zero) crystallographic defects and impurities. My initial hope was that, as a result, there would be only very weak damping of mechanical vibrations in monocrystalline NEMS. But as we shrink mechanical devices, we repeatedly find that acoustic energy loss seems to increase in proportion to the increasing surface-to-volume ratio. This result clearly implicates surfaces in the devices' vibrational energy-loss processes. In a state-of-the-art silicon beam measuring 10 nanometers wide and 100 nanometers long, more than 10 percent of the atoms are at or next to the surface. It is evident that these atoms will play a central role, but understanding precisely how will require a major, sustained effort.

In this context, nanotube structures, which have been heralded lately, look ideal. A nanotube is a crystalline, rodlike material perfect for building the miniature vibrating structures of interest to us. And because it has no chemical groups projecting outward along its length, one might expect that interaction with "foreign" materials at its surfaces would be minimal. Apparently not. Although nanotubes exhibit ideal characteristics when shrouded within pristine, ultra-high vacuum environments, samples in more ordinary conditions, where they are exposed to air or water vapor, evince electronic properties that are markedly different. Mechanical properties are likely to show similar sensitivity. So surfaces definitely *do* matter. It would seem there is no panacea.

# Payoff in the Glitches

Futuristic thinking is crucial to making the big leaps. It gives us some wild and crazy goals—a holy grail to

## Taking Charge

### SINGLE ELECTRONICS

Advances in nanofabrication allowed Theodore A. Fulton and Gerald J. Dolan to build a single-electron transistor at Bell Laboratories in 1987. In this structure, the controlled movement of individual electrons through a nanodevice was first achieved.

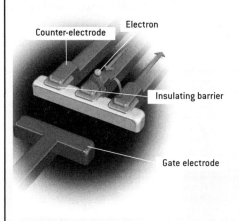

At its heart was a coulomb island, a metallic electrode isolated from its counter-electrodes by thin insulating oxide barriers (*diagram*). The counter-electrodes led up to the macroscale laboratory instrumentation used to carry out the experiments. An additional gate electrode was offset from the coulomb island by a small gap; it allowed direct control of the charge introduced to the island. Electric current flowed through the device from one counter-electrode to another, as in a conventional circuit, but here it was limited by the stepwise hopping of electrons onto and off the coulomb island.

Fulton and Dolan's experiments demonstrate both the fundamental physics of single-electron charging and the potential of these devices as ultrasensitive electrometers: instruments that can easily detect individual electron charges. Circuits that switch one electron at a time could someday form the basis for an entirely new class of nanoelectronics. The advent of such single electronics, however, also presages problems that will have to be faced as conventional electronic circuits are shrunk to the nanoscale.

chase. And the hope of glory propels us onward. Yet the famous 19th-century chemist Friedrich August Kekulé once said, "Let us learn to dream, gentlemen, then perhaps we shall find the truth. . . . But let us beware of publishing our dreams before they have been put to the proof by the waking understanding."

This certainly holds for nanoscience. While we keep our futuristic dreams alive, we also need to keep our expectations realistic. It seems that every time we gain access to a regime that is a factor of 10 different—and presumably "better"—two things happen. First, some wonderful, unanticipated scientific phenomenon emerges. But then a thorny host of underlying, equally unanticipated new problems appear. This pattern has held true as we have pushed to decreased size, enhanced sensitivity, greater spatial resolution, higher magnetic and electric fields, lower pressure and temperature, and so on. It is at the heart of why projecting forward too many orders of magnitude is usually perilous. And it is what should imbue us with a sense of humility and proportion at this, the beginning of our journey. Nature has already set the rules for us. We are out to understand and employ her secrets.

Once we head out on the quest, nature will frequently hand us what initially seems to be nonsensical, disappointing, random gibberish. But the science in the glitches often turns out to be even more important than the grail motivating the quest. And being proved the fool in this way can truly be the joy of doing science. If we had the power to extrapolate everything correctly from the outset, the pursuit of science would be utterly dry and mechanistic. The delightful truth is that, for complex systems, we do not, and ultimately probably cannot, know everything that is important.

Complex systems are often exquisitely sensitive to a myriad of parameters beyond our ability to sense and record—much less control—with sufficient regularity and precision. Scientists have studied, and in large part already understand, matter down to the fundamental particles that make up the neutrons, protons and electrons that are of crucial importance to chemists, physicists and engineers. But we still cannot deterministically predict how arbitrarily complex assemblages of these three elemental components will finally behave en masse. For this reason, I firmly believe that it is on the foundation of the experimental science already under way, in intimate collaboration with theory, that we will build the road to true nanotechnology. Let's keep our eyes open for surprises along the way!

## More to Explore

**Nanoelectromechanical Systems Face the Future.** Michael Roukes in *Physics World*, Vol. 14, No. 2; February 2001. Available at **physicsweb.org/article/world/14/2/8**

The author's group: **www.its.caltech.edu/~nano**

Richard Feynman's original lecture "There's Plenty of Room at the Bottom" can be found at **www.its.caltech.edu/~feynman**

# The Author

*MICHAEL ROUKES,* professor of physics at the California Institute of Technology, heads a group studying nanoscale systems. Among the holy grails his team is chasing are a potential billionfold improvement in present-day calorimetry, which would allow observation of the individual heat quanta being exchanged as nanodevices cool, and a potential quadrillion-fold increase in the sensitivity of magnetic resonance imaging, which would enable complex biomolecules to be visualized with three-dimensional atomic resolution.

# "The Nanodrive
## 2. Project"

by Peter Vettiger and Gerd Binnig

*Inventing a nanotechnology device for mass production
and consumer use is trickier than it sounds*

M any engineers have had the thrill of designing a novel product that then enters mass production and pops up all over the world. We hope—in fact, we would lay better than 50–50 odds on it—that within three years we will experience the rarer pleasure of having launched an entirely new class of machine.

Nanotechnology is much discussed these days as an emerging frontier, a realm in which machines operate at scales of billionths of a meter. Research on microelectromechanical systems (MEMS)—devices that have microscopic moving parts made using the techniques of computer chip manufacture—has similarly produced a lot of hype and yet relatively few commercial products. But as we can attest, having spent six years so far on one of the first focused projects to create a nanomechanical device suitable for mass production, at such tiny scales, engineering is inextricably melded with scientific research. Unexpected obstacles appear on the road from a proof-of-principle experiment to a working prototype and then on to a product that succeeds in the marketplace.

MAKING TRACKS: Arrays of cantilever-mounted tips inscribe millions of digital bits on a plastic surface in an exceedingly small space.

Here at IBM we call our project Millipede. If we stay on track, by 2005 or so you will be able to buy a postage stamp–size memory card for your digital camera or portable MP3 player. It will hold not just a few dozen megabytes of video or audio, as typical flash memory cards do, but several gigabytes—sufficient to store an entire CD collection of music or several feature films. You will be able to erase and rewrite data to the card. It will be quite fast and will require moderate amounts of power. You might call it a nanodrive.

That initial application may seem interesting but hardly earth-shaking. After all, flash memory cards with a gigabyte of capacity are already on the market. The impressive part is that Millipede stores digital data in a completely different way from magnetic hard disks, optical compact discs and transistor-based memory chips. After decades of spectacular progress, those mature technologies have entered the home stretch; imposing physical limitations loom before them.

The first nanomechanical drives, in contrast, will barely scratch the surface of their potential. Decades of refinements will lie ahead. In principle, the digital bits that future generations of Millipede-like devices will write, read and erase could continue to shrink until they are individual molecules or even atoms. As the moving parts of the nanodrives get smaller, they will

## Overview/Millipede Project

- Today's digital storage devices are approaching physical limits that will block additional capacity. The capabilities of the Millipede "nanodrive"—a micro-mechanical device with components in the nano-size range—could take off where current technologies will end.
- Millipede uses grids of tiny cantilevers to read, write and erase data on a polymer media. The cantilever tips poke depressions into the plastic to make digital 1's; the absence of a dent is a digital 0.
- The first Millipede products, most likely postage stamp–size memory cards for portable electronic devices, should be available within three years.

work faster and use power more efficiently. The first products to use Millipede technology will most likely be high-capacity data storage cards for cameras, mobile phones and other portable devices. The nanodrive cards will function in much the same way as the flash memory cards in these devices today but will offer several-gigabyte capacity for lower cost. The same technology might also be a tremendous boon to materials science research, biotechnology or even applications that are not currently foreseeable.

It was this long-term promise that got us so excited half a dozen years ago. Along the way, we learned that sometimes the only way around a barrier is a serendipitous discovery. Fortunately, besides unexpected obstacles, there are also unexpected gifts. It seems there often is a kind of reward from nature if one dares enter new areas. On the other hand, sometimes nature is not so kind, and you must overcome the difficulty yourself. We have worked hard on such problems but not too hard. If at one stage we had no idea how to address an issue, perhaps a year later we found an answer. Good intuition is required in such cases, in which you expect the problem can be solved, although you do not yet know how.

## A Crazy Idea

In a way, Millipede got its start on a soccer field. The two of us played on the soccer team of the IBM Zurich Research Laboratory, where we work. We were introduced by another teammate, Heinrich Rohrer. Rohrer had started at the Zurich lab in 1963, the same year as one of us (Vettiger); he had collaborated with the other one (Binnig) on the invention in 1981 of the scanning tunneling microscope (STM), a technology that led to the long-sought ability to see and manipulate individual atoms.

In 1996 we were both looking for a new project in a considerably changed environment. The early 1990s had been a tough time for IBM, and the company had sold off its laser science effort, the technology part of which was managed by Vettiger. Binnig had closed his satellite lab in Munich and moved back to Zurich. Together with Rohrer, we started brainstorming ways to apply STM or other scanning probe techniques, specifically atomic force microscopy (AFM), to the world beyond science.

AFM, invented by Binnig and developed jointly with Christoph Gerber of the Zurich lab and Calvin F. Quate of Stanford University, is the most widely used local probe technique. Like STM, AFM took a radically new approach to microscopy. Rather than magnifying objects by using lenses to guide beams of light or by bouncing electrons off the object, an AFM slowly drags or taps a minuscule cantilever over an object's surface. Perched on the end of the cantilever is a sharp tip tapered to a width of less than 20 nanometers— a few hundred atoms. As the cantilever tip passes over the dips and rises in the surface (either in contact with or in extreme proximity to it), a computer translates the deflection of the lever into an image, revealing, in the best cases, each passing atom.

While Binnig was making the first images of individual silicon atoms in the mid-1980s, he inadvertently kept bumping the tip into the surface, leaving little dents in the silicon. The possibility of using an STM or AFM as an atomic-scale data storage device was obvious: make a dent for a 1, no dent for a 0. But the difficulties were clear, too. The tip has to follow the contours of the medium mechanically, so it must scan very slowly compared with the high-speed rotation of a hard-disk platter or the nanosecond switching time of transistors.

Other pros and cons soon became apparent. Because of the extremely small mass of the cantilevers, AFM operation with the tip in direct contact with the medium is much faster than that of an STM or a noncontact AFM, though still not as fast as magnetic storage. On the other hand, tips of a contact AFM wear quickly when used to scan metal surfaces. And—perhaps most important—once the tip has made a dent, there was no obvious way to "erase" it.

A group led by Dan Rugar at the IBM Almaden Research Center in San Jose, Calif., had tried shooting laser pulses at the tip to heat it; that would in turn soften the plastic so the tip could dent it. The group was able to create compact disc–like recordings that stored data more densely than even today's digital video discs (DVDs) do. It also performed extensive wear tests with very promising results. But the system was too slow, and it still lacked a technique to erase and rewrite data.

## How the Nanodrive Works

The Millipede Nanodrive prototype operates like a tiny phonograph, using the sharp tips of minuscule silicon cantilevers to read data inscribed in a polymer medium. An array of 4,096 levers, laid out in rows with their tips pointing upward, is linked to control microcircuitry that converts information encoded in the analog pits into streams of digital bits. The polymer is suspended on a scanning table by silicon leaf springs, which permits tiny magnets (*not shown*) and electromagnetic coils to pan the storage medium across a plane while it is held level over the tips. The tips contact the plastic because the levers flex upward by less than a micron.

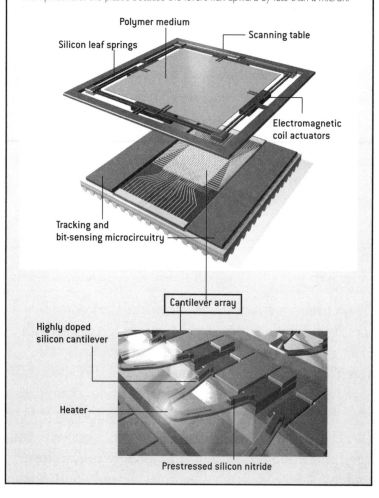

Polymer medium

Scanning table

Silicon leaf springs

Electromagnetic coil actuators

Tracking and bit-sensing microcircuitry

Cantilever array

Highly doped silicon cantilever

Heater

Prestressed silicon nitride

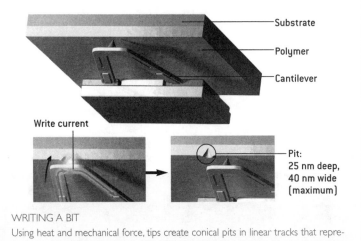

WRITING A BIT

Using heat and mechanical force, tips create conical pits in linear tracks that represent series of digital 1's. To produce a pit, electric current travels through the lever, heating a doped region of silicon at the end to 400 degrees Celsius, which allows the prestressed lever structure to flex into the polymer. The absence of a pit is a 0.

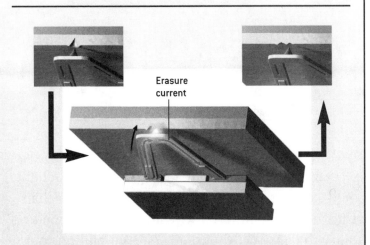

ERASING A BIT

The latest Millipede prototype erases an existing bit by heating the tip to 400 degrees C and then forming another pit just adjacent to the previously inscribed pit, thus filling it in (shown). An alternative erasure method involves inserting the hot tip into a pit, which causes the plastic to spring back to its original flat shape.

## How the Nanodrive Works *(continued)*

READING A BIT

To read data, the tips are first heated to about 300 degrees C. When a scanning tip encounters and enters a pit (*top*), it transfers heat to the plastic. Its temperature and electrical resistance thus fall, but the latter by only a tiny amount, about one part in a few thousand. A digital signal processor converts this output signal, or its absence, into a data stream (*bottom*).

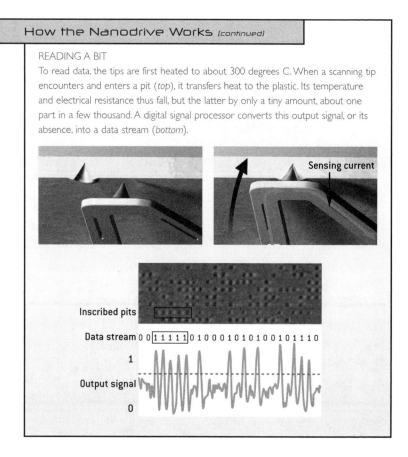

Our team sketched out a design that we thought could supply these missing ingredients. Rather than using just one cantilever, why not exploit chipmakers' ability to construct thousands or even millions of identical microscopic parts on a thumbnail-size slice of silicon? Working together in parallel—like the legs of a millipede—an army of slow AFM tips could read or write data quite rapidly.

Here more imagination was required to envision a chance for success than to come up with the idea itself. Although operating a single AFM is sometimes difficult, we were confident that a massively parallel device incorporating many tips would have a realistic chance of functioning reliably.

As a start, we needed at least one way to erase, be it elegant or not. Alternatives, we thought, might pop up later. We developed a scheme of erasing large fields of bits. We heated them above the temperature at which the polymer starts to flow, in much the same way as the surface of wax gets smooth when warmed by a heat gun. Although the technique worked nicely, it was somewhat complicated because, before erasing a field, all the data that were to be retained had to be transferred into another field. (Later on, as we'll explain, nature presented a much better method.)

With these rough concepts in mind, we started our journey into an interdisciplinary project. With the pair of us working in one team, we bridged two IBM departments, physics and devices. (They were eventually merged into a single science and technology department.) We were also joined by Evangelos Eleftheriou and his team, from our laboratory's communication systems department. Today several other groups from within IBM Research and from universities collaborate with us.

When different cultures meet, misunderstandings cannot be prevented, at least not in the beginning. We, however, experienced a huge benefit from mixing disparate viewpoints.

## 99 Percent Perspiration . . .

We were not MEMS experts, and researchers in the MEMS and scanning probe technology communities had so far dismissed our project as harebrained. Although others, such as Quate's group at Stanford, were working at that time on STM- or AFM-based data storage, ours was the only project committed to large-scale integration of many probes. We hoped to achieve a certain vindication by presenting a working prototype in January 1998 at the IEEE 11th International Workshop on Micro-Electro-Mechanical Systems in Heidelberg, Germany. Instead we had a nearly working prototype to show. We presented a five-by-five array of tips in an area of 25 square millimeters.

It was able to demonstrate parallel imaging, but parallel writing failed. We had overlooked a niggling but critical technical detail: the wires leading to the heaters were metallic and too thin to handle the current passing through them. They immediately blew like overloaded fuses because of the phenomenon of elec-tromigration in metal films. Electromigration was well described in the literature, and we should have known about it. This was not our only mistake, but in our group mistakes can be admitted and quickly corrected.

Despite the setbacks, our lab's managers sensed real progress. They allowed us to double the size of our team to eight. We had learned from the 25-tip array that the aluminum wiring had to be replaced—which we did with highly doped silicon cantilevers. We also found that it was possible to level out the tip array below the storage medium with high precision in a relatively large area, which made us confident enough to move to a bigger array right away.

Vettiger recognized one serious problem in May 1998 as he was giving an invited talk at the IBM Almaden lab. He was describing how the cantilevers would be arranged in regular rows and columns, all of them connected to a grid of electrical wires. But as he was explaining how this system would work, he suddenly realized that it wouldn't. Nothing would stop the electric current from going everywhere at once; there would thus be no way to reliably send a signal to an individual cantilever.

The uncontrolled flow of current is actually a well-known phenomenon when units in an array have to be addressed through columns and rows. A common solution is to attach a transistor switch to each unit. But putting transistors on the same chip at the tips was not an option; the tips must be sharpened under intense heat that would destroy tiny transistors. Back at the lab, we tried all kinds of tricks to improve control of the current flow—none of which pleased Vettiger. The bigger the array, the more serious this flaw became. A quick calculation and simulation by Urs Dürig of our team showed that for an array of 1,000 units, addressing single cantilevers for writing would still be possible; reading the small signals of individual levers, however, would fail.

Vettiger slept poorly that night, fretting. The team was just about to complete the chip design for a 1,024-tip array. Vettiger told them to wait. For days the team agonized over the problem, until at last Vettiger and Michel Despont saw a practical answer: place a Schottky diode (an electrical one-way street) next to each cantilever. This highly nonlinear device would block the undesired current from flowing into all the other cantilevers. We reworked the design and soon had a 32-by-32-tip array, our second prototype.

This prototype proved that many of our ideas would work. All 1,024 cantilevers in the array came out intact and bent up by just the right amount so that they applied the correct amount of force when mated to a soft polymer medium called PMMA, which is mounted on a separate chip called a scanning table. Copper electromagnetic coils placed behind the scanning table were able to keep the PMMA surface from tilting too much as it panned left, right, back and forward atop the cantilever tips. (A new media scanner designed by Mark Lantz and Hugo Rothuizen has since reduced vibration sensitivity, which was then a problem.) Each 50-micron-long cantilever had a little resistor at its end. An electrical pulse sent through the tip heated it to around 400 degrees Celsius for a few microseconds.

The initial results with our second prototype were encouraging. More than 80 percent of the 1,024 levers worked properly on first pass, and there was only one narrow "dark" zone crossing the center of the storage field, resulting from a twisting of the chip when it was mounted. Not in our wildest dreams did we expect such success at this early stage of the project.

## From R to D

In the five-by-five device, each lever had at its base a piezoresistive sensor that converted mechanical strain to a change in resistance, allowing the system to detect when the tip had dropped into a pit—a digital 1. We began exploring approaches to detect pits more definitively. We ran tests with Schottky diodes integrated into the cantilevers, hoping that the strain would modify their resistance. Somehow the diodes did not have the expected properties. We nonetheless observed a strong signal when a bit was sensed. After some head-scratching, we found the surprising reason. It turned out to be a thermal phenomenon. If the cantilever is preheated to about 300 degrees C, not quite hot enough to make a dent, its electrical resistance drops significantly whenever the tip falls into a pit [*see illustration on page 36*]. We never would have thought to use a thermal effect to measure a motion, deflection or position. On macro scales, doing so would be too slow and unreliable because of convection—the circulatory motion that occurs in a fluid medium, in this case air, as heat is transferred between two objects of different temperatures. On the micro scale, however, turbulence does not exist, and hotter and cooler objects reach equilibrium within microseconds.

Although this result was unexpected, it was very useful. Now we could use the same heater on each lever for reading bits as well as writing them. Instead of three or four wires per cantilever, only two would be needed.

We presented this second prototype at the 1999 IEEE MEMS conference. This time the other researchers in attendance were more impressed. But what really excited upper managers at IBM were pictures of regular rows of pits that Millipede had written into the polymer. The pits were spaced just 40 nanometers apart—about 30 times the density of the best hard drives then on the market.

Shortly thereafter, in early 2000, the Millipede project changed character. We began focusing more on producing a storage system prototype. The team grew to about a dozen workers. We again brought together two departments, with Eleftheriou and his team joining us. They contributed their unique expertise in recording-channel technology, which they had been applying to magnetic recording very successfully. They began developing the electronic part of a fully functional system prototype—from basic signal processing and error-correction coding to complete system architecture and control.

We had just discovered a way to erase a small area, and in cooperation with Eleftheriou, we could even turn it into a system in which no erasing is required before overwriting. In the new, local erasure method, when the tip temperature is high enough to soften the material, surface tension and the springiness of the polymer cause a pit to pop up again. Instead of annealing a larger field using a heater integrated into the storage substrate—as in the block erasure method described earlier—the tip heats the medium locally. Because of electrostatic forces, a certain loading force on the tip cannot be avoided. So when the tip is heated to a high enough temperature and a new indentation is produced, older bits in close proximity are erased at the same time. If a row of pits is written densely, each newly created bit will eliminate the previous one, and only the last bit in the row will remain. This mechanism can even be used to overwrite old data with new code without knowing what the old one was. In a marriage of our experience in physics with Eleftheriou's recording-channel expertise, we developed a special form of constrained coding for such direct overwriting.

At that point it was clear that the team needed to work on the speed and power efficiency of Millipede. We had to start measuring signal-to-noise ratios, bit error rates and other indicators of how well the nanodrive could record digital data. And we had to choose a size and shape for the nanodrive. The "form factor" can be all-important in the consumer electronics marketplace, specifically in the mobile area, which we had chosen to address first.

## The Road Ahead

In the last months of 2002 our group put the final touches on the third-generation prototype, which has 4,096 cantilevers arranged in a 64-by-64 array that measures 6.4 millimeters on a side. Cramming more levers onto a chip is challenging but doable. Today we could fabricate chips with one million levers, and 250 such arrays could be made from a standard 200-millimeter wafer of silicon. The primary task now is to strike the right balance between two desiderata. First, our design for a complete nanodrive system—not just the array and the scanning table but also the integrated microelectronics that control them—should be inexpensive enough to be immediately competitive and, especially for handheld devices, operable at low power. But it is critical that the system function dependably despite damage that occurs during years of consumer use.

We have found polymers that work even better than PMMA does. In these plastics, pits appear to be stable for at least three years, and a single spot in the array can be written and erased 100,000 times or more. But we are less sure about how the tips will hold up after making perhaps 100 billion dents over several years of operation. Dürig and Bernd Gotsmann of our team are working closely with colleagues at IBM Almaden to modify existing polymers or develop new ones that meet the requirements for our storage application.

And although human eyes scanning an image of the Millipede medium can easily pick out which blocks in the grid contain pits and which do not, it is no trivial matter to design simple electronic circuitry that does the same job with near-perfect accuracy. Detecting which bits represent 0's and which are 1's is much easier if the pits are all the same depth and are evenly spaced along straight tracks. That means that the scanning table must be made flat, held parallel to the tips and panned with steady speed in linear motion—all to within a few nanometers' tolerance. Just recently, we learned that by suspending the scanning table on thin leaf springs made of silicon, we gain much better control of its movement. Even so, we will add an active feedback system that is very sensitive to the relative position of the two parts to meet such nanoscopic tolerances while the device is jostling around on a jogger's waistband.

Any mechanical system such as Millipede that generates heat has to cope with thermal expansion. If the polymer medium and the silicon cantilevers differ by more than about a single degree C, the alignment of the bits will no longer match that of the tips. A feedback system to compensate for misalignment would add complexity and thus cost. We are not yet certain of the best solution to this problem.

Fortunately, nature has helped again. Millipede and the storage substrate carrying the polymer film are both made from silicon and will therefore expand by the same amount if they are at the same temperature. Additionally, the gap between the tip array and the substrate is so small that the air trapped between them acts as an excellent heat conductor, and a temperature difference between them is hardly achievable.

Because the project has now matured to the point that we can begin the first steps toward product development, our team has been joined by Thomas R. Albrecht,

# High-Density Memory Projects

IBM's Millipede Project is only one of several efforts to bring compact, high-capacity computer memories to market.

| COMPANY | DEVICE TECHNOLOGY | MEMORY CAPACITY | COMMERCIALIZATION |
|---|---|---|---|
| Hewlett-Packard<br>*Palo Alto, Calif.* | Thumbnail-size atomic force microscope (AFM) device using electron beams to read and write data onto recording area | At least a gigabyte (GB) at the outset | End of the decade |
| Hitachi<br>*Tokyo* | AFM-based device; specifics not disclosed | Has not been revealed | Has not been revealed |
| Nanochip<br>*Oakland, Calif.* | AFM-tipped cantilever arrays that store data on a silicon chip | Half a GB at first; potential for 50 GBs | Expected in 2004 |
| Royal Philips Electronics<br>*Eindhoven,<br>the Netherlands* | Optical system similar to rerecordable CDs using a blue laser to record and read data on a three-centimeter-wide disk | Up to a GB per side, perhaps 4 GBs in all | Expected in 2004 |
| Seagate Technology<br>*Scotts Valley, Calif.* | Rewritable system using AFM or other method, operating on a centimeter-size chip | As many as 10GBs on a chip for portables | Expected in 2006 or later |

a data storage technologist from IBM Almaden who helped to shepherd IBM's Microdrive to market. Bringing the Microdrive from the lab to the customer was a journey similar to what Millipede may face in the next few years.

For the members of our group, this transition to product development means that we will surrender the Millipede more and more to the hands of others. Stepping back is the most difficult part and, at the same time, the most critical to the success of a project.

Indeed, we cannot yet be certain that the Millipede program will result in a commercial device. Although we scientists no longer consider this a high-risk project, we still rejoice when a new prototype works. If we are lucky, our newest prototypes will reveal problems that our team knows how to fix.

In any case, we are excited that, at a minimum, this nanomechanical technology could allow researchers for the first time to scan a square centimeter of material with near-atomic resolution. So far the project has generated close to 30 relatively basic patents. No one knows whether nanodrives will make it in the market. But they will be a new class of machine that is good for something, and for us that is its own reward.

## More to Explore

**In Touch with Atoms.** Gerd Binnig and Heinrich Rohrer in *Reviews of Modern Physics*, Vol. 71, No. 2, pages S324–S330; March 1999.

**The "Millipede"—Nanotechnology Entering Data Storage.** P. Vettiger, G. Cross, M. Despont, U. Drechsler, U. Dürig, B. Gotsmann, W. Häberle, M. A. Lantz, H. E. Rothuizen, R. Stutz and G. Binnig in *IEEE Transactions on Nanotechnology*, Vol. 1, No. 1, pages 39–55; March 2002.

For more about nanotechnology in IBM Research and elsewhere, see **www.research.ibm.com/pics/nanotech/**

## The Authors

*PETER VETTIGER* and *GERD BINNIG* have collaborated extensively to refine technologies for the

Millipede nanodrive concept. Vettiger has had a long-standing career as a technologist specializing in microfabrication and nanofabrication. He joined the IBM Zurich Research Laboratory in 1963 and graduated in 1965 with a degree in communications technology and electronics engineering from the Zurich University of Applied Sciences. His academic career culminated in an honorary Ph.D. awarded in 2001 by the University of Basel. Binnig completed his Ph.D. in physics in 1978 at the Johann Wolfgang Goethe University in Frankfurt, Germany, and joined the Zurich lab that same year. His awards for outstanding scientific achievements include the 1986 Nobel Prize for Physics, which he received together with Heinrich Rohrer for the invention of the scanning tunneling microscope.

# Innovations:
# 3. "Nano Patterning"
## by Gary Stix

*IBM brings closer to reality chips that put themselves together*

Self-assembly has become a critical implement in the toolbox of nanotechnologists. Scientists and engineers who explore the nano realm posit that the same types of forces that construct a snowflake—the natural attractions and repulsions that prompt molecules to form intricate patterns—can build useful structures— say, medical implants or components in electronic chips. So far much of the work related to self-assembling nanostructures has been nothing more than demonstrations in university laboratories. To go beyond being a scientific curiosity, these nanotech materials and techniques will have to get from benchtop to a $2-billion semiconductor fabrication facility.

Four years ago two members of the technical staff at the IBM Thomas J. Watson Research Center in Yorktown Heights, N.Y., began to contemplate how they might transform the vision of self-assembly into a practical reality. The collaborators, Charles Black and Kathryn Guarini, knew that the grand academic ambitions of making an entire set of chip circuits from self-assembly had to be set aside. Instead the best way

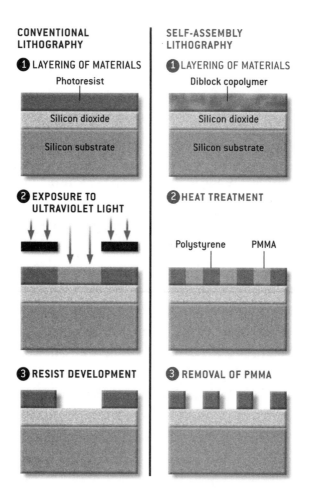

**CONVENTIONAL LITHOGRAPHY**

**1 LAYERING OF MATERIALS**
Photoresist
Silicon dioxide
Silicon substrate

**2 EXPOSURE TO ULTRAVIOLET LIGHT**

**3 RESIST DEVELOPMENT**

**SELF-ASSEMBLY LITHOGRAPHY**

**1 LAYERING OF MATERIALS**
Diblock copolymer
Silicon dioxide
Silicon substrate

**2 HEAT TREATMENT**
Polystyrene    PMMA

**3 REMOVAL OF PMMA**

OLD AND NEW: Conventional lithography exposes a photoresist to ultraviolet light. An etchant then removes the exposed part of the photoresist. Self-assembly patterning occurs when a diblock copolymer is heated, thereby separating the two polymers in the material into defined areas before the PMMA is etched away. The template of cylindrical holes is transferred into the silicon dioxide before the holes are filled with nanocrystalline silicon used to store data (steps not shown).

to begin, they thought, might be to replace a single manufacturing step. "The idea was that if we could ease the burden in any of the hundreds of steps to make a chip, we should take advantage of that," Black says.

They first had to select what type of molecules might self-construct without disrupting routine silicon manufacturing practices. Polymers were an obvious choice. They make up the "resist" used in photolithography— the material that, once exposed to ultraviolet or shorter-wavelength light, is washed away to form a circuit pattern. During the first two years of their quest, the duo spent time learning about polymers and the optimal temperatures and thicknesses at which they would self-assemble. They built on the work of Craig J. Hawker of the IBM Almaden Research Center in San Jose, Calif., and that of former IBMer Thomas P. Russell, a polymer scientist at the University of Massachusetts at Amherst. Both had done research on how polymers self-assemble on silicon. With this knowledge, Black and Guarini even started making things.

The two researchers appeared at conferences, giving presentations about honeycomb patterns that had self-assembled. But that accomplishment consisted of little more than PowerPoints, the type of through-the-microscope images found in abundance at any academic conference on nanotechnology. What would the nano patterns be good for? How could they be integrated into a fabrication line? Could they best circuit-patterning techniques that had already received hundreds of millions of dollars of investment?

Finally, last year, the pair demonstrated how a self-assembled honeycomb pattern might work in a real manufacturing facility. The material chosen for the demo was a diblock copolymer, one in which two polymers—in this case, polystyrene (Styrofoam) and polymethylmethacrylate (Plexiglas, or PMMA)—are tied together by chemical bonds. When spun onto the surface of a rotating silicon wafer, the two polymers separate, as if they were oil and water. Although the molecules stretch out, the chemical bonds keep them attached. Subsequent heat treatment exacerbates this elongation. In the end, PMMA ends up concentrated in small cylinders surrounded on all sides by the

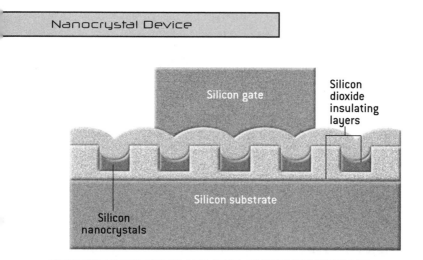

**Nanocrystal Device**

FLASH MEMORY: A layer of self-assembled silicon nanocrystals is inserted into an otherwise standard device as part of a novel IBM manufacturing process.

polystyrene. The diblock copolymer thus forms on its own into a nearly complete honeycomblike template.

To finish creating the 20-nanometer-wide pores, an organic etching solvent removes the PMMA. A subsequent etching step transfers the same honeycomb pattern into an underlying layer of more robust silicon dioxide. Then a coating of amorphous silicon gets deposited across the surface of the wafer. A gas etches away the silicon except for that deposited in the holes. All that is left are nanocrystalline cylinders surrounded by silicon dioxide. The final steps place an insulating layer and a block of silicon atop the structure, the block forming a "gate" that turns the electronic device off and on. Black and Guarini's honeycomb results in a nanostructure that is part of a working flash-memory device, the kind that retains digital bits even when a camera or a voice recorder is turned off. The nanocrystalline cylinders form capacitors where data are stored.

Manufacturing engineers are leery of introducing new technologies unless a researcher can make a very good case for their adoption. Self-assembly potentially fits the bill. Creating closely spaced holes for a flash memory would prove exceedingly difficult with ordinary lithographic and deposition methods. Forming nanocrystals using conventional techniques creates elements of different sizes that are all jumbled together. In contrast, the self-assembled nanocrystals are evenly spaced and of uniform size, improving their durability and their capacity to retain a charge while allowing the cylinders to shrink to smaller than 20 nanometers.

The IBM demonstration served as proof of principle in the strictest sense of the expression. The company has not made commercial flash memories for years, so the invention could not be applied immediately to improve its own manufacturing operations. But the nanocrystals enabled the pair of researchers to flaunt this type of nano patterning. "Politically in the company maybe it wasn't the smartest demonstration we could have done, but everybody was supportive and could see the power of the technology," Black says.

The understanding gained of how to integrate nanomanufacturing with conventional chipmaking may provide new approaches to fabricating other IBM electronic components. Making holes and filling them could create "decoupling" capacitors recessed into the chip substrate that smooth out fluctuations in the power supplied to a chip.

Using a variant of nano patterning, a self-assembling polymer could also create tiny, finger-shaped silicon protrusions sticking up from the underlying substrate. These fingers would constitute the "channel" in a transistor through which electrons flow—but one in which electrons flow vertically instead of across a chip, as in today's devices. The gate to turn the transistor off and on could encircle the silicon finger. The geometry might prevent electrons from "tunneling," or leaking, through the channel when the transistor is in the off state, a constant threat when feature sizes become very small.

Ultimately, self-assembly might play a much bigger role in fashioning electronic circuits. But the incrementalist approach of Black and Guarini may represent the most promising way to get nanotechnology adopted as a real manufacturing tool. "The greatest excitement is that these materials aren't just in the polymer-science laboratory anymore," Black says. A small step for small manufacturing.

# 4. "The First Nanochips"

by G. Dan Hutcheson

*As scientists and engineers continue to push back the limits of chipmaking technology, they have quietly entered into the nanometer realm*

For most people, the notion of harnessing nanotechnology for electronic circuitry suggests something wildly futuristic. In fact, if you have used a personal computer made in the past few years, your work was most likely processed by semiconductors built with nanometer-scale features. These immensely sophisticated microchips—or rather, nanochips—are now manufactured by the millions, yet the scientists and engineers responsible for their development receive little recognition. You might say that these people are the Rodney Dangerfields of nanotechnology. So here I would like to trumpet their accomplishments and explain how their efforts have maintained the steady advance in circuit performance to which consumers have grown accustomed.

The recent strides are certainly impressive, but, you might ask, is semiconductor manufacture really nanotechnology? Indeed it is. After all, the most widely accepted definition of that word applies to something with dimensions smaller than 100 nanometers, and the first transistor gates under this mark went into production in 2000. Integrated circuits coming to market now have gates that are a scant 50 nanometers wide. That's 50 billionths of a meter, about a thousandth the width of a human hair.

Having such minuscule components conveniently allows one to stuff a lot into a compact package, but saving space per se is not the impetus behind the push for extreme miniaturization. The reason to make things small is that it lowers the unit cost for each transistor. As a bonus, this overall miniaturization shrinks the size of the gates, which are the parts of

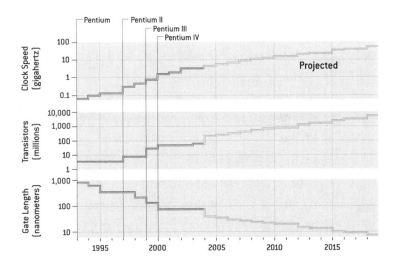

MICROPROCESSOR components have entered the nano realm during the past decade, as illustrated by the evolution of Intel's Pentium series (*black*), which shows remarkable gains in the speed and quantity of transistors, both of which rise as the gate length of the transistors diminishes. If the semiconductor industry even comes close to matching its forecasts (*gray*), these trends should continue.

the transistors that switch between blocking electric current and allowing it to pass. The more narrow the gates, the faster the transistors can turn on and off, thereby raising the speed limits for the circuits using them. So as microprocessors gain more transistors, they also gain more speed.

The desire for boosting the number of transistors on a chip and for running it faster explains why the semiconductor industry, just as it crossed into the new millennium, shifted from manufacturing microchips to making nanochips. How it quietly passed this milestone, and how it continues to advance, is an amazing story of people overcoming some of the greatest engineering challenges of our time—challenges every bit as formidable as those encountered in building the first atomic bomb or sending a person to the moon.

## Straining to Accelerate

The best way to get a flavor for the technical innovations that helped to usher in the current era of nanochips is to survey improvements that have been made in each of the stages required to manufacture a modern semiconductor—say, the microprocessor that powers the computer on which I typed this text. That chip, a Pentium 4, contains some 42 million transistors intricately wired together. How in the world was this marvel of engineering constructed? Let us survey the steps.

Before the chipmaking process even begins, one needs to obtain a large crystal of pure silicon. The traditional method for doing so is to grow it from a small seed crystal that is immersed in a batch of molten silicon. This process yields a cylindrical ingot— a massive gem-quality crystal—from which many thin wafers are then cut.

It turns out that such single-crystal ingots are no longer good enough for the job: they have too many "defects," dislocations in the atomic lattice that hamper the silicon's ability to conduct and otherwise cause trouble during chip manufacture. So chipmakers now routinely deposit a thin, defect-free layer of single-crystal silicon on top of each wafer by exposing it to a gas containing silicon. This technique improves the speed of the transistors, but engineers have been pushing hard to do even better using something called silicon-on-insulator technology, which involves putting a thin layer of insulating oxide slightly below the surface of the wafer. Doing so lowers the capacitance (the ability to store electrical charge) between parts of the transistors and the underlying silicon substrate, capacitance that would otherwise sap speed and waste power. Adopting a silicon-on-insulator geometry can boost the rate at which the transistors can be made to switch on and off (or, alternatively, reduce the power needed) by up to 30 percent. The gain is equivalent to what one gets in moving one generation ahead in feature size.

IBM pioneered this technology and has been selling integrated circuits made with it for the past five years. The process IBM developed, dubbed SIMOX, short for separation by *im*plantation of *ox*ygen, was to bombard the silicon with oxygen atoms (or rather, oxygen ions, which have electrical charge and can thus be readily accelerated to high speeds). These ions implant themselves deep down, relatively speaking, where they combine with atoms in the wafer and form a layer of silicon dioxide. One difficulty with this approach is that the passage of oxygen ions through the silicon creates many defects, so the surface has to be carefully heated afterward to mend disruptions to the crystal lattice. The greater problem is that oxygen implantation is inherently slow, which makes it costly. Hence, IBM reserved its silicon-on-insulator technology for its most expensive chips.

A new, faster method for accomplishing the same thing is, however, gaining ground. The idea is to first form an insulating oxide layer directly on top of a silicon wafer. One then flips the oxidized surface over and attaches it onto another, untreated wafer. After cleverly pruning off most of the silicon above the oxide layer, one ends up with the desired arrangement: a thin stratum of silicon on top of the insulating oxide layer on top of a bulk piece of silicon, which just provides physical support.

The key was in developing a precision slicing method. The French company that did so, Soitec, aptly trademarked the name Smart Cut for this technique, which requires shooting hydrogen ions through the oxidized surface of the first wafer so that they implant themselves at a prescribed depth within the underlying silicon. (Implanting hydrogen can be done more rapidly than implanting oxygen, making this process relatively inexpensive.) Because the hydrogen ions do most of their damage right where they stop, they produce a level within the silicon that is quite fragile. So after flipping this treated wafer over and attaching it to a wafer of bulk silicon, one can readily cleave the top off at the weakened plane. Any residual roughness in the surface can be easily polished smooth. Even IBM now employs Smart Cut for making some of its high-performance chips, and AMD (Advanced Micro Devices in Sunnyvale, Calif.) will use it in its upcoming generation of microprocessors.

The never-ending push to boost the switching speed of transistors has also brought another very basic change to the foundations of chip manufacture, something called strained silicon. It turns out that forcing the crystal lattice of silicon to stretch slightly (by about 1 percent) increases the mobility of electrons passing through it considerably, which in turn allows the transistors built on it to operate faster. Chipmakers induce strain in silicon by bonding it to another crystalline material—in this case, a silicon-germanium blend—for which the lattice spacing is greater. Although the technical details of how this strategy is being employed remain closely held, it is well known that many manufacturers are adopting this approach. Intel, for example, is using strained silicon in an advanced version of its Pentium 4 processor called Prescott, which began selling late last year.

## Honey, I Shrunk the Features

Advances in the engineering of the silicon substrate are only part of the story: the design of the transistors constructed atop the silicon has also improved tremendously in recent years. One of the first steps in the fabrication of transistors on a digital chip is growing a thin layer of silicon dioxide on the surface of a wafer, which is done by exposing it to oxygen and water vapor, allowing the silicon, in a sense, to rust (oxidize). But unlike what happens to the steel body of an old car, the oxide does not crumble away from the surface. Instead it clings firmly, and oxygen atoms required for further oxidization must diffuse through the oxide coating to reach fresh silicon underneath. The regularity of this diffusion provides chipmakers with a way to control the thickness of the oxide layers they create.

For example, the thin oxide layers required to insulate the gates of today's tiny transistors can be made by allowing oxygen to diffuse for only a short time. The problem is that the gate oxide, which in modern chips is just several atoms thick, is becoming too slim to lay down reliably. One fix, of course, is to make this layer thicker. The rub here is that as the thickness of the oxide increases, the capacitance of the gate decreases. You might ask: Isn't that a good thing? Isn't capacitance bad? Often capacitance is indeed something to be avoided, but the gate of a transistor operates by inducing electrical charge in the silicon below it, which provides a channel for current to flow. If the capacitance of the gate is too low, not enough charge will be present in this channel for it to conduct.

The solution is to use something other than the usual silicon dioxide to insulate the gate. In particular, semiconductor manufacturers have been looking hard at what are known as high-K (high-dielectric-constant) materials, such as hafnium oxide and strontium titanate, ones that allow the oxide layer to be made thicker, and thus more robust, without compromising the ability of the gate to act as a tiny electrical switch.

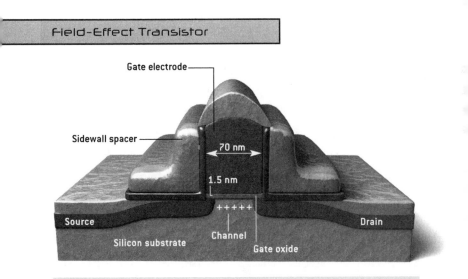

**Field-Effect Transistor**

Gate electrode

Sidewall spacer

70 nm

1.5 nm

+ + + + +

Source

Drain

Channel

Silicon substrate

Gate oxide

The fundamental building block of a microprocessor is the field-effect transistor, which acts as a simple switch. The proper voltage applied to the gate electrode induces charge along the channel, which then carries current between the source and the drain, turning the switch on. With sufficiently small gates, these transistors can switch on and off billions of times each second.

Placing a high-K insulator on top of silicon is, however, not nearly as straightforward as just allowing it to oxidize. The task is best accomplished with a technique called atomic-layer deposition, which employs a gas made of small molecules that naturally stick to the surface but do not bond to one another. A single-molecule-thick film can be laid down simply by exposing the wafer to this gas long enough so that every spot becomes covered. Treatment with a second gas, one that reacts with the first to form the material in the coating, creates the molecule-thin veneer. Repeated applications of these two gases, one after the next, deposit layer over layer of this substance until the desired thickness is built up.

After the gate insulator is put in place, parts of it must be selectively removed to achieve the appropriate pattern on the wafer. The procedure for doing so (lithography) constitutes a key part of the technology needed to create transistors and their interconnections. Semiconductor lithography employs a photographic mask to generate a pattern of light and shadows, which is projected on a wafer after it is coated with a light-sensitive substance called photoresist. Chemical processing and baking harden the unexposed photoresist, which protects those places in shadow from later stages of chemical etching.

Practitioners once believed it impossible to use lithography to define features smaller than the wavelength of light employed, but for a few years now, 70-nanometer features have been routinely made using ultraviolet light with a wavelength of 248 nanometers.

## Basic Chipmaking Process

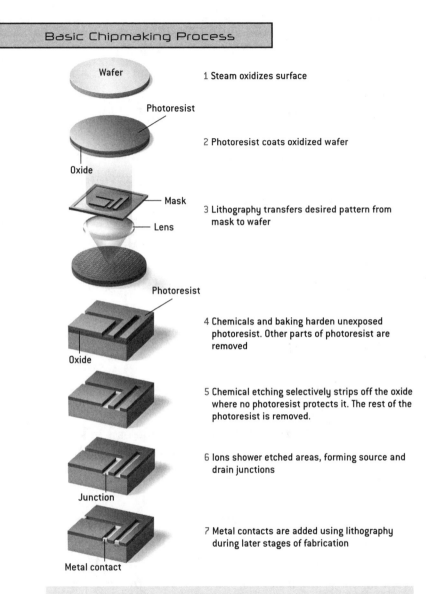

Wafer

1 Steam oxidizes surface

Photoresist

Oxide

2 Photoresist coats oxidized wafer

Mask

Lens

3 Lithography transfers desired pattern from mask to wafer

Photoresist

Oxide

4 Chemicals and baking harden unexposed photoresist. Other parts of photoresist are removed

5 Chemical etching selectively strips off the oxide where no photoresist protects it. The rest of the photoresist is removed.

6 Ions shower etched areas, forming source and drain junctions

Junction

7 Metal contacts are added using lithography during later stages of fabrication

Metal contact

A circular wafer of silicon about the size of a dinner plate provides the starting point for the step-by-step chipmaking process, which sculpts transistors and their interconnections. Some of the manipulations shown below are repeated many times in the course of production, to build complex structures one layer at a time.

To accomplish this magic, lithography had to undergo some dramatic changes. The tools brought to bear have complicated names—optical proximity correction, phase-shifting masks, excimer lasers—but the idea behind them is simple, at least in principle. When the size of the features is smaller than the wavelength of the light, the distortions, which arise through optical diffraction, can be readily calculated and corrected for. That is, one can figure out an arrangement for that mask that, after diffraction takes place, yields the desired pattern on the silicon. For example, suppose a rectangle is needed. If the mask held a plain rectangular shape, diffraction would severely round the four corners projected on the silicon. If, however, the pattern on the mask were designed to look more like a dog bone, the result would better approximate a rectangle with sharp corners.

This general strategy now allows transistors with 50-nanometer features to be produced using light with a wavelength of 193 nanometers. But one can push these diffraction-correction techniques only so far, which is why investigators are trying to develop the means for higher-resolution patterning. The most promising approach employs lithography, but with light of much shorter wavelength—what astronomers would call "soft" x-rays or, to keep with the preferred term in the semiconductor industry, extreme ultraviolet.

Semiconductor manufacturers face daunting challenges as they move to extreme ultraviolet lithography, which reduces the wavelengths (and thus the size of the

## Slicing a Nanochip

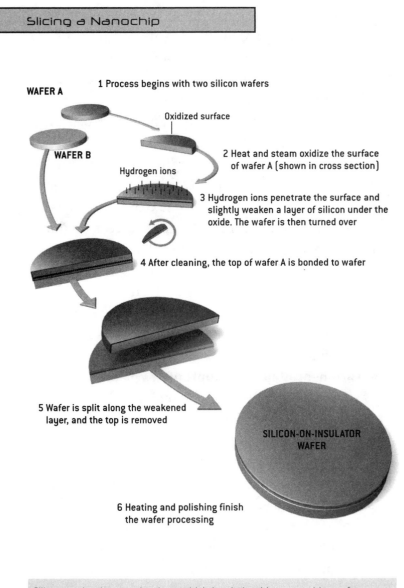

**WAFER A**

1 Process begins with two silicon wafers

Oxidized surface

**WAFER B**

2 Heat and steam oxidize the surface of wafer A (shown in cross section)

Hydrogen ions

3 Hydrogen ions penetrate the surface and slightly weaken a layer of silicon under the oxide. The wafer is then turned over

4 After cleaning, the top of wafer A is bonded to wafer

5 Wafer is split along the weakened layer, and the top is removed

**SILICON-ON-INSULATOR WAFER**

6 Heating and polishing finish the wafer processing

Silicon-on-insulator technology, which has helped improve chip performance considerably, has become cheaper and easier to adopt, thanks to a technique called Smart Cut, developed by Soitec, a French company.

features that can be printed) by an order of magnitude. The prototype systems built so far are configured for a 13-nanometer wavelength. They are truly marvels of engineering—on both macroscales and nanoscales.

Take, for instance, the equipment needed to project images onto wafers. Because all materials absorb strongly at extreme ultraviolet wavelengths, these cameras cannot employ lenses, which would be essentially opaque. Instead the projectors must use rather sophisticated mirrors. For the same reason, the masks must be quite different from the glass screens used in conventional lithography. Extreme ultraviolet work demands masks that absorb and reflect light. To construct them, dozens of layers of molybdenum and silicon are laid down, each just a few nanometers thick. Doing so produces a highly reflective surface onto which a patterned layer of chromium is applied to absorb light in just the appropriate places.

As with other aspects of chipmaking, these masks must be free from imperfections. But because the wavelengths are so small, probing for defects proves a considerable challenge. Scientists and engineers from industry, academe and government laboratories from across the U.S. and Europe are collaboratively seeking solutions to this and other technical hurdles that must be overcome before extreme ultraviolet lithography becomes practical. But for the time being, chipmakers must accept the limits of conventional lithography and maintain feature sizes of at least 50 nanometers or so.

Using lithography to imprint such features on a film of photoresist is only the first in a series of manipulations used to sculpt the wafer. Process engineers must also figure out how to remove the exposed parts of the photoresist and to etch the material that is uncovered in ways that do not eat into adjacent areas. And one must be able to wash off the photoresist and the residues left over after etching—a mundane task that becomes rather complicated as the size of the features shrinks.

The problem is that, seen at the nanometer level, the tiny features put on the chip resemble tall, thin skyscrapers, separated by narrow chasms. At this scale, traditional cleaning fluids act as viscous tidal waves and could easily cause things to topple. Even if that catastrophe can be avoided, these liquids have a troubling tendency to get stuck in the nanotechnology canyons.

An ingenious solution to this problem emerged during the 1990s from work done at Los Alamos National Laboratory: supercritical fluids. The basic idea is to use carbon dioxide at elevated pressure and temperature, enough to put it above its so-called critical point. Under these conditions, $CO_2$ looks something like a liquid but retains an important property of a gas—the lack of viscosity. Supercritical carbon dioxide thus flows easily under particles and can mechanically dislodge them more effectively than can any wet chemical. (It is no coincidence that supercritical carbon dioxide has recently become a popular means

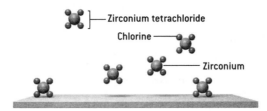

1 The surface is exposed to the first of two gases, here zirconium tetrachloride (ZrCl$_4$).

2 Molecules of ZrCl$_4$ adhere to the surface but not to one another.

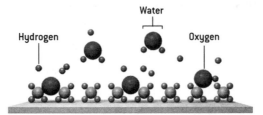

3 The coated surface is exposed to a second gas, in this case steam (H$_2$O).

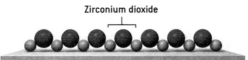

4 The ZrCl$_4$ on the surface reacts with the water (H$_2$O) to form a single-molecule-thick veneer of the desired material, zirconium dioxide (ZrO$_2$).

Atomic-layer deposition allows chipmakers to lay down coatings that are extremely thin. Cycling through these steps repeatedly builds up the coating— one molecule of thickness at a time.

to dry-clean clothes.) And mixed with the proper co-solvents, supercritical carbon dioxide can be quite effective in dissolving photoresist. What is more, once the cleaning is done, supercritical fluids are easy to remove: lowering the pressure—say, to atmospheric levels—causes them to evaporate away as a normal gas.

With the wafer cleaned and dried in this way, it is ready for the next step: adding the junctions of the transistors—tubs on either side of the gate that serve as the current "source" and "drain." Such junctions are made by infusing the silicon with trace elements that transform it from a semiconductor to a conductor. The usual tactic is to fire arsenic or boron ions into the surface of the silicon using a device called an ion implanter. Once emplaced, these ions must be "activated," that is, given the energy they need to incorporate themselves into the crystal lattice. Activation requires heating the silicon, which often has the unfortunate consequence of causing the arsenic and boron to diffuse downward.

To limit this unwanted side effect, the temperature must be raised quickly enough that only a thin layer on top heats up. Restricting the heating in this way ensures that the surface will cool rapidly on its own. Today's systems ramp up and down by thousands of degrees a second. Still, the arsenic and boron atoms diffuse too much for comfort, making the junctions thicker than desired for optimum speed. A remedy is, however, on the drawing board—laser thermal processing, which can vary the temperature at a rate of up to five *billion* degrees a second. This technology, which should soon break out of the lab and onto the factory floor, holds the promise of preventing virtually all diffusion and yielding extremely shallow junctions.

Once the transistors are completed, millions of capacitors are often added to make dynamic random-access memory, or DRAM. The capacitors used for DRAM have lately become so small that manufacturing engineers are experiencing the same kinds of problems they encounter in fashioning transistor gates. Indeed, here the problems are even more urgent, and the answer, again, appears to be atomic-layer deposition, which was adopted for the production of the latest generation of DRAM chips.

## New Meets Old

Atomic-layer deposition can also help in the next phase of chip manufacture, hooking everything together. The procedure is to first lay down an insulating layer of glass on which a pattern of lines is printed and etched. The grooves are then filled with metal to form the wires. These steps are repeated to create six to eight layers of crisscrossing interconnections. Although the semiconductor industry has traditionally used aluminum for this bevy of wires, in recent years it has shifted to copper, which allows the chips to operate faster and helps to maintain signal integrity. The problem is that copper contaminates the junctions, so a thin conductive

## Extreme Ultraviolet Lithography

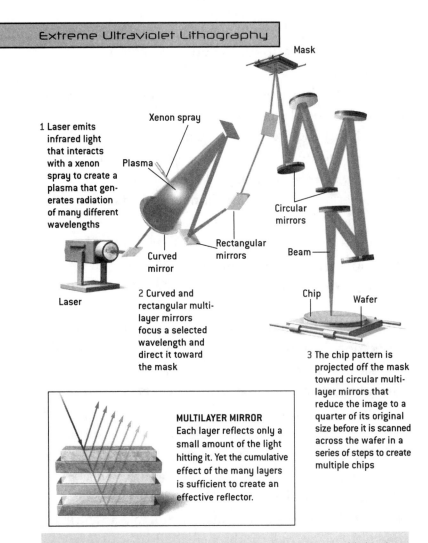

**Mask**

**1** Laser emits infrared light that interacts with a xenon spray to create a plasma that generates radiation of many different wavelengths

**Xenon spray**

**Plasma**

**Circular mirrors**

**Curved mirror**

**Rectangular mirrors**

**Beam**

**Laser**

**2** Curved and rectangular multilayer mirrors focus a selected wavelength and direct it toward the mask

**Chip**

**Wafer**

**3** The chip pattern is projected off the mask toward circular multilayer mirrors that reduce the image to a quarter of its original size before it is scanned across the wafer in a series of steps to create multiple chips

**MULTILAYER MIRROR**
Each layer reflects only a small amount of the light hitting it. Yet the cumulative effect of the many layers is sufficient to create an effective reflector.

Lenses, which are used in conventional lithography systems, would absorb the extreme ultraviolet light required for patterning features smaller than 50 nanometers. As a result, lithography systems may soon use multilayer mirrors instead of lenses to focus extreme ultraviolet radiation from a plasma and to reduce the size of the image projected from the mask. This illustration is based on one of the design concepts under consideration by the Dutch manufacturer ASML.

barrier (one that does not slow the chip down) needs to be placed below it. The solution was atomic-layer deposition.

The switch to copper also proved challenging for another reason: laying down copper is inherently tricky. Many high-tech approaches were attempted, but none worked well. Then, out of frustration, engineers at IBM tried an old-fashioned method: electroplating, which leaves an uneven surface and has to be followed with mechanical polishing. At the time, the thought of polishing a wafer—that is, introducing an abrasive grit—was anathema to managers in this industry, which is downright obsessed with cleanliness. Hence, the engineers who originally experimented with this approach at IBM did so without seeking permission from their supervisor. They were delighted to discover that the polishing made the wafer more amenable to lithographic patterning (because the projection equipment has a limited depth of focus), that it removed troublesome defects from the surface and that it made it easier to deposit films for subsequent processing steps.

The lesson to be learned here is that seemingly antiquated methods can be just as valuable as cutting-edge techniques. Indeed, the semiconductor industry has benefited a great deal in recent years from combinations of old and new. That it has advanced as far as it has is a testament to the ingenious ability of countless scientists and engineers to continually refine the basic method of chip manufacture, which is now more than four decades old.

Will the procedures used for fabricating electronic devices four decades down the road look anything like those currently employed? Although some futurists would argue that exotic forms of nanotechnology will revolutionize electronics by midcentury, I'm betting that the semiconductor industry remains pretty much intact, having by then carried out another dazzling series of incremental technical advances, ones that are today beyond anyone's imagination.

## More to Explore

**Toward Point One.** Gary Stix in *Scientific American*, Vol. 272, No. 2, pages 90–95; February 1995.

**Technology and Economics in the Semiconductor Industry.** G. Dan Hutcheson and Jerry D. Hutcheson in *Scientific American*, Vol. 274, No. 1, pages 54–62; January 1996.

**Handbook of Semiconductor Manufacturing Technology.** Edited by Yoshio Nishi and Robert Doering. Marcel Dekker, 2000.

2003 International Technology Roadmap for Semiconductors. Available online at **http:// public.itrs.net/Files/2003ITRS/Home2003.htm**

News from International SEMATECH, a global consortium of leading semiconductor manufacturers, is available online at **www.sematech.org**

# The Author

*G. DAN HUTCHESON* is chief executive officer and president of VLSI Research Inc., a market research and economic analysis firm serving the semiconductor industry. Hutcheson, who holds a master's degree in economics from San Jose State University, has constructed various quantitative models that chipmakers can use to forecast costs and to guide them in procuring equipment. As an industry analyst, he follows the emerging technologies of semiconductor manufacture and provides summaries of the latest research advances and manufacturing trends to interested companies.

# "Nanotechnology and
## 5. the Double Helix"

by Nadrian C. Seeman

*DNA is more than just the secret of life—it is also a versatile component for making nanoscopic structures and devices*

The year 2003 witnessed the 50th anniversary of the discovery of DNA's double-helix structure by James D. Watson and Francis H. Crick. Their discovery reduced genetics to chemistry and laid the foundations for the next half a century of biology. Today thousands of researchers are hard at work deciphering the myriad ways that genes control the development and functioning of organisms. All those genes are written in the medium that is DNA.

Yet this extraordinary molecule has other uses in addition to those of biochemistry. By employing the techniques of modern biotechnology, we can make long DNA molecules with a sequence of building blocks chosen at will. That ability opens the door to new paths not taken by nature when life evolved. In 1994, for example, Leonard M. Adleman of the University of Southern California demonstrated how DNA can be used as a computational device [see "Computing with DNA," by Leonard M. Adleman; SCIENTIFIC AMERICAN, August 1998]. In this article I will discuss another nonbiological use of DNA: the building of structures and devices whose essential

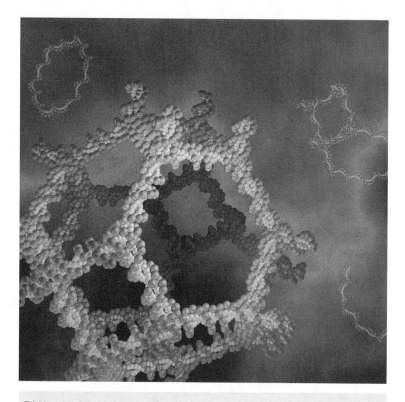

DNA strands self-assemble into a complicated structure when their base sequences are designed to pair up with specific partners. Here a stick model of a truncated octahedron, which has six square faces and eight hexagonal faces, has formed. The edges are about 20 nanometers long. A short "hairpin" of DNA sticks out from each corner. The hairpins could be modified to link truncated octahedra together to form a regular three-dimensional scaffold.

elements and mechanisms range from around one to 100 nanometers in size—in a word, nanotechnology.

Such structures have many potential applications. Regular lattices made of DNA could hold copies of large biological molecules in an ordered array for x-ray crystallography to determine their structure, an important step in the "rational" design of drugs. Alternatively, the lattices could serve as scaffolding for nanoelectronic components, either as a working device or as a step in the manufacture of a device. Materials could be constructed—either made of the DNA or made by it—with structures precisely designed at the molecular level. DNA machines with moving parts could be employed as nanomechanical sensors, switches and tweezers as well as for more elaborate robotic functions.

## Branched DNA

The nanoscale is the scale of molecules. A typical bond between two atoms is about 0.15 nanometer long. (A nanometer is a billionth of a meter.) The helix of DNA has a diameter of about two nanometers, and it twists full circle once every 3.5 nanometers or so, a distance of about 10 base pairs, which form the "rungs" of DNA's ladder [*see illustration on page 82*]. A short piece of DNA has highly specific interactions with other chemicals, depending on its sequence of base pairs. One can imagine using such pieces to recognize particular molecules or to control the composition of a material by acting as a catalyst. And for many years biologists have used DNA for its recognition properties, especially exploiting the "sticky ends" in genetic engineering. A sticky end occurs when one strand of the helix extends for several unpaired bases beyond the other [*see illustration on page 84*]. The stickiness is the propensity of the overhanging piece to bond with a matching strand that has the complementary bases in the corresponding order—the base adenine on one strand pairs with thymine on the opposite strand, and cytosine binds with guanine. [For another application using the stickiness of DNA, see "The Magic of Microarrays," by Stephen H. Friend and Roland B. Stoughton; SCIENTIFIC AMERICAN, February 2002.]

At first sight, it does not appear that DNA can lead to interesting structures. Naturally occurring DNA forms a linear chain, like a long piece of twine, so that all one can envision making from it is lines or circles, perhaps snarled up or knotted in one way or another. But a linear chain is not the only form that DNA takes. During certain cellular processes, DNA exists briefly as a branched molecule. This branching occurs when DNA replicates (in preparation for cell division) and during recombination (when genetic material is swapped between matching pairs of chromosomes, as happens when sperm and eggs are produced).

## Overview/DNA Nanotech

- DNA is an ideal molecule for building nanometer-scale structures. Strands of DNA can be programmed to self-assemble into complex arrangements by producing the strands with the appropriate combinations of complementary bases, which preferentially bond together to form stretches of double helices.
- DNA scaffolds could hold guest molecules in orderly arrays for crystallography. They could also hold molecule-size electronic devices, or be used to build materials with precise molecular configurations.
- Nanometer-scale DNA machines can function by having parts of their structure change from one DNA conformation to another. These movements can be controlled by chemical means or by the use of special DNA strands.

The branches form when the double helix partially unravels into two strands. In replication, each strand is made into a new double helix by the addition of complementary nucleotides all along its length. (A nucleotide is the combination of a base and the corresponding section of the backbone of the helix.) More interesting is the crossover that occurs in recombination, in which two pieces of DNA break and partially unravel and the resulting four strands join up somewhat like the intersection where two highways cross.

In recombining DNA, the branch point occurs where each of the four strands switches from one partner to another. The branch point moves around because of twofold symmetry (like that of the numeral "69") in the base sequences that flank it. This symmetry means that each strand can pair up with either of two other strands. In 1979 I was working with Bruce H. Robinson, now at the University of Washington, to describe the nature of this motion when I recognized that synthetic DNA molecules lacking this symmetry could form branched molecules whose branch points do not move. To design such a junction, one would make four strands of DNA. For each strand, the sequence along half of the strand would match half of a second strand and the remaining half would match half of a third strand [*see illustration on page 84*].

DNA's favorite structure is the conventional double helix identified by Watson and Crick. A quantity called free energy determines which structure is favored. In general, free energy determines whether a chemical

## The Structure of DNA

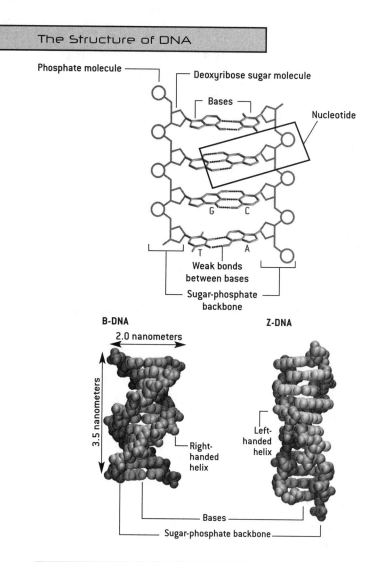

Phosphate molecule

Deoxyribose sugar molecule

Bases

Nucleotide

G    C

T         A

Weak bonds
between bases

Sugar-phosphate
backbone

**B-DNA**

2.0 nanometers

3.5 nanometers

Right-
handed
helix

**Z-DNA**

Left-
handed
helix

Bases

Sugar-phosphate backbone

DNA is a nanoscale structure, consisting of a double backbone of phosphate and sugar molecules between which complementary pairs of bases (A and T; C and G) are connected by weak bonds (top). DNA's most common conformation is B-DNA (bottom left), which twists in a right-handed double helix about two nanometers in diameter. One full turn of the helix is about 3.5 nanometers, or 10 to 10.5 base pairs long. In special circumstances DNA can form a left-handed double helix called Z-DNA (bottom right).

reaction proceeds in the forward or reverse direction; it also determines the conformation—the folds and joins—of large molecules such as DNA, RNA and proteins. A chemical system always tends to change toward the state that has the lowest free energy. For two complementary strands of nucleotides, the free energy is minimized when they pair up to form a double helix.

The four strands of our immobile junction can come together and form the maximum amount of conventional DNA double helices only by forming a branched molecule. In general, a branch point is not favored—it increases the free energy of the molecule—but this increase is outweighed by the much greater energy saving in the four arms made of ordinary double-helix DNA. Today it is simple to synthesize such strands and implement this idea of a stable branched DNA molecule, but in 1979 it was state-of-the-art chemistry and I was a crystallographer, not an organic chemist, so mostly I just thought about the system. (It was not until 1982 that I learned how to make DNA.)

## Inspiration from Escher

I figured out that it ought to be possible to make branched DNA junctions with many arms, not just four. One day, in the fall of 1980, I went over to the campus pub to think about six-arm junctions. For some reason, I thought about Dutch artist M. C. Escher's woodcut *Depth*. I realized that the center of each fish in that picture was just like an idealized picture of the

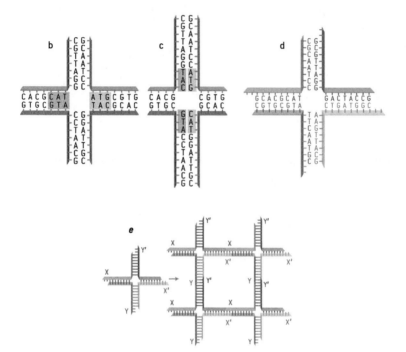

Self-assembly of DNA structures is enabled by the strong propensity of DNA strands with complementary base sequences to cohere to one another and form a double helix. So-called sticky ends (a), short strands of unpaired DNA extending from one end of a DNA molecule, join specific units together. A second key building block is branched DNA (b), in which three or more helices are joined at a branch point. In naturally occurring branched DNA, the branch point can move around (c) because the base sequences on the four arms are symmetrical. Artificial branched DNA that lacks that symmetry has a fixed branch point (d). Copies of branched DNA with complementary sticky ends (e) self-assemble into a lattice structure.

branch point of a six-arm junction. Six features extend from that center point on the fish: a head and a tail, a top fin and bottom fin, a left fin and a right fin. The fish are organized in the same way as the molecules in a molecular crystal, with regular repeats forward and back, up and down, left and right. It struck me that if I held junctions together using sticky ends, I might be able to organize matter on the nanometer scale in the same way that Escher held his school of fish together using his imagination.

We have several good reasons for wanting to build such structures. First, we are aiming to fabricate macroscopic pieces of matter made of designed molecules joined together in a structure that is controlled with nanoscopic precision. This procedure could result in materials having novel properties or novel combinations of properties. For example, materials with designed optical properties, such as photonic crystals, could be made by constructing precisely defined arrays with specific repeat distances [see "Photonic Crystals: Semiconductors of Light," by Eli Yablonovitch; SCIENTIFIC AMERICAN, December 2001].

Another goal is to use DNA as scaffolding to hold other molecules in arrays, including those that do not form a regular crystalline structure on their own. In this way, one could make crystals for use in crystallography experiments by making DNA cages that contain large biological molecules such as proteins within them [*see illustration on page 87*]. Such cages would enable crystallographers to determine the three-dimensional structures of the enclosed molecules—a key procedure in the rational design of drugs that mesh precisely with specific parts of a targeted molecule. (This crystallographic application is the one that most strongly motivates my interest in this field.) Currently many of the receptor molecules that could be excellent drug targets do not lend themselves to conventional crystallography. In a similar fashion, one could organize nanoelectronic components into very small memory devices, as Robinson and I suggested in 1987. My group has not used DNA as scaffolding yet, but we have had many other successes that are steps on the way to achieving this goal.

Why use DNA for these purposes? The chief reason is that strands of DNA interact in the most programmable and predictable way. A sticky end that is $N$ bases long has one of $4^N$ possible sequences of bases. This enormous variability and the propensity of the end to bond to only a closely matching sequence provide ample scope for designing molecules that consist of a large number of DNA strands joined to one another in a completely specified manner. Furthermore, we know that two sticky ends form the classic helical DNA structure when they cohere, and these helical stretches of DNA are relatively stiff. Thus, we know not only which strands link to which other strands but also the detailed shape of the joined segments. We do not have such specific information for proteins or antibodies, which are other candidates for working elements. Those also have tremendous variability, but determining what shape a protein will take and how two proteins or

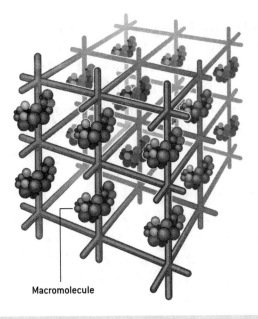

**Macromolecule**

Escher's woodcut *Depth* inspired the author to consider an array of six-arm junctions connected together to form a three-dimensional molecular crystal. The center of each fish is just like the branch point of a six-arm junction. Instead of arms, six features extend from that center point: a head and a tail, a top and bottom fin, and a left and right fin. Molecular scaffolding could hold other molecules in regular arrays. For example, DNA cages containing oriented biological macromolecules as guests could be used in crystallography experiments. In a similar fashion, nanoelectronic components could be organized into very small memory devices.

antibodies will join together are laborious problems that would have to be solved anew for each example.

Another reason for working with DNA is the simplicity of its synthesis with the tools of the biotechnology industry. We can manipulate DNA with many enzymes, such as restriction enzymes (which cleave DNA at particular sites) or ligases (which catalyze the joining of two molecules by covalent bonds—sturdy chemical bonds that involve the sharing of pairs of electrons between atoms). These tools can be used to make and manipulate conventional DNA, as well as exotic derivatives, in which different bases from the usual four are incorporated or in which additional molecules are attached on the outside of the DNA's backbone (the sides of the DNA ladder). Medical researchers hoping to use nucleic acids (DNA and RNA) for therapy have made many such variants. DNA is extremely well suited to making such derivatives because every nucleotide along the helix has sites where molecules can be attached.

Finally, as we will see below, DNA can be induced to form structures different from the standard double helix. We can build nanomechanical devices whose parts move—such as closing tweezers or a rotating shaft—when there is a transition from one DNA structure to another. One drawback is that DNA objects must be constructed in an aqueous solution. It is no problem, however, to dry the resulting structures (on mica, for instance) as we do to make microscopic images of our results.

## Stick Models

The first step in any new scientific research program is to establish the basic feasibility of the project. In 1991 Junghuei Chen, now at the University of Delaware, and I did this by building a DNA molecule shaped like a cube formed from sticks [see illustration on page 90].

Each edge of the cube is a stretch of double-helical DNA; each corner is a three-arm junction. Each corner is connected to three other corners; it is said that the cube's connectivity is three. Genetic engineers had made many linear DNA constructs, but this was the first DNA molecule with connectivity greater than two. The cube self-assembles from pieces of DNA designed to adhere to one another, but the ends of each piece do not join up. Ligases can connect these free ends, resulting in six closed loops, one for each face of the cube. Because of the helical nature of DNA, each of these loops is twisted around the loops that flank it, so the cube cannot come apart, even if all the bonds joining the base pairs together were somehow broken.

Yuwen Zhang, now at Baxter Healthcare, and I built another shape called a truncated octahedron, which is similar to but more complicated than a cube [*see illustration on page 90*]. Although three-arm junctions would have sufficed to make individual truncated octahedra, instead we built them using four-arm junctions. We intended that the extra arm sticking out at each corner could be used to connect truncated octahedra together in a larger structure, but in the end we did not continue in this direction. We had created only a very tiny quantity of truncated octahedra—enough to characterize their structure but too few to attempt to join them together—and even that minute sample had taken us to the limits of what we could do without overhauling our procedures (for example, by robotizing repetitive steps). Instead we turned to simpler components.

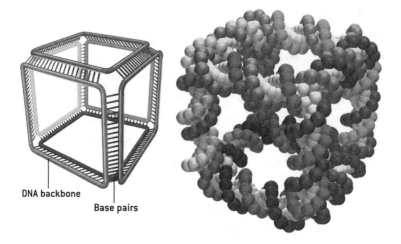

DNA backbone

Base pairs

Stick cube (*right*) made out of six loops of DNA demonstrated that three-dimensional structures can be built. The backbone of each DNA strand is depicted as colored spheres (a different color for each strand) and the bases as white spheres. Each edge of the cube comprises 20 nucleotide pairs, or about two complete turns of the double helix. Each corner is a three-arm junction. Simplified schematic (*left*) depicts how the DNA strands are connected but omits the helical twists.

Another reason for changing direction was that along the way we realized that the stick polyhedra we had built were not rigid. DNA is a stiff molecule: a stretch of DNA that is two or three turns long (the lengths we use for the polyhedra edges) can wiggle around its helix's axis no more than a piece of cooked spaghetti two or three millimeters long can wiggle around its central axis. That inflexibility ensured that the edges of our stick figures were rigid, but we learned that the angles at each corner were quite variable. The polyhedra we had built were rather like structures made of toothpicks stuck into blobs of marshmallow at the corners. Such structures might have uses, but building a regular lattice is not one of them. It is much easier to self-assemble an orderly, crystallike piece of matter from bricklike components than from marshmallows.

To solve this problem, my group examined another branched motif found in biological recombination systems, the DNA double-crossover (DX) molecule. The DX molecule consists of two double helices aligned side by side, with strands crossing between the helices, yoking them together [*see box on page 92*]. We characterized this molecule and established that it is stiff. We also demonstrated that a DX molecule containing another small double helical region (called a DX + J molecule) is very stiff. This additional double helical region creates a bump on the top of the DX molecule, which serves as a marker—a nanotech equivalent of a dab of paint.

In collaboration with Erik Winfree of the California Institute of Technology, Furong Liu and Lisa A. Wenzler of my group at New York University used combinations of DX and DX + J molecules as tiles to make two-dimensional crystals with defined patterns. The tiles are joined together by sticky ends on each helix. One arrangement, with columns of DX tiles alternating with columns of DX + J tiles, produces a pattern of stripes separated by about 32 nanometers. We deposited the arrays on a flat mica surface and examined them with an atomic-force microscope to confirm that the structure had the correct dimensions. We established that the pattern was not accidental by making a second crystal with modified tiles that link together with three

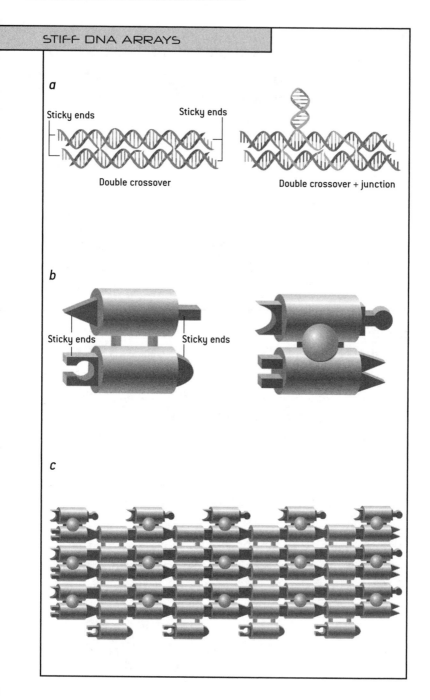

STIFF DNA ARRAYS

*a*

Sticky ends

Sticky ends

Double crossover

Double crossover + junction

*b*

Sticky ends

Sticky ends

*c*

Two-dimensional crystals can be made out of stiff bricks of DNA. The bricks (*a*) are double-crossover (DX) and double-crossover-plus-junction (DX + J) units, which cannot flop around at their joining points the way that multiarm junctions can. Each brick has four distinct sticky ends for joining bricks together. The extended green strand of the DX + J unit sticks out of the plane. Each unit is about 4 by 16 nanometers in size. For simplicity, the DX and DX + J units are shown schematically, with geometric shapes at their ends representing the sticky ends (*b*). In a solution, the sticky ends cohere and the units self-assemble in a two-dimensional pattern (*c*). The striped pattern shows up in an atomic-force microscope image of the crystal (*d*) (which is deposited onto a flat mica surface for the microscopy). The bright stripes, spaced about 32 nanometers apart, are the lines of DNA protruding from the DX + J units. Parallelograms of DNA have also been self-assembled into two-dimensional patterns (*e*, *f*).

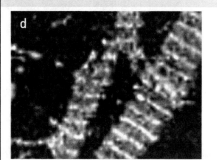

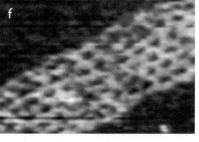

DX columns for each DX + J column, to produce stripes with double the separation.

Recently John H. Reif's group at Duke University demonstrated "DNA bar codes" made using such patterns. In these tilings, the positions of stripes were programmed to occur in a pattern representing the number "01101" (with molecules analogous to our DX and DX + J serving as 0 and 1, respectively). The pattern was programmed using an input DNA strand whose sequence encoded the 01101 pattern. The analogues of the DX and DX + J bricks self-assembled on the sections of the DNA strand corresponding to 0 and 1, respectively. Many such five-brick sequences then joined up in parallel, generating the 01101 pattern of stripes. The stripes were about 15 nanometers apart. By examining the stripes with an atomic-force microscope, one is effectively using the bar code to read out the data that were encoded on the input DNA strand. This visual means of reading out the DNA sequence could greatly speed up the readout stage of DNA-based computing and might also be used for mapping mutations.

Chengde Mao, now at Purdue University, and I have made two-dimensional patterns from DNA parallelograms similar to our stick polyhedra. Copies of this unit can be joined to form a crystal that extends like a waffle in two dimensions. One can tune the sizes of the cavities in the array by changing the dimensions of the parallelograms. Although individual branched junctions are floppy, arranging four of them at the corners of a parallelogram results in a well-behaved unit in a parallelogram array.

## Nanomachines

Central to nanotechnology are molecular-scale machines. DNA has proved to be very useful for constructing these machines. We have built several devices from DNA, but here I will focus on two that have well-defined structures. In both cases, the mechanism is based on a structural transition of DNA molecules—a change from one conformation (such as the usual double helix) to another.

Conventional DNA is a right-handed helix. Imagine walking up a spiral staircase with your left hand on the inner banister and your right hand on the outer one. Such a staircase is a right-handed helix. Conventional right-handed DNA is called B-DNA and is the most energetically favored structure in typical aqueous conditions.

Double-helical DNA can also assume a number of different structures depending on its base sequence and the chemical species present in the solution in which it is immersed. One is Z-DNA, whose structure was first characterized in 1979 by Alexander Rich and his colleagues at the Massachusetts Institute of Technology [*see illustration on page 82*]. Z-DNA is a left-handed DNA structure.

To make Z-DNA typically requires a stretch of alternating cytosine and guanine bases. The DNA backbone includes negatively charged phosphate groups, and these come close together in the Z-DNA structure. This formation is favored only if the charges of the phosphates can be screened from one another by an aqueous environment containing either a high concentration of salt or a special "effector" species, such as cobalt hexammine, $Co(NH_3)_6^{+++}$, that does the same job at a much lower concentration. The cytosine-guanine sequence requirement lets us control *where* on a DNA molecule the B-Z transition takes place (and hence *what* our machine does), and the environmental requirement lets us control *when* the transition (and hence the machine action) occurs.

My N.Y.U. colleagues Weiqiong Sun and Zhiyong Shen, Mao and I built a device consisting of two DX molecules connected by a shaft of double-helical DNA. In the middle of the shaft is a sequence of 20 pairs that can adopt the Z-structure in the appropriate conditions. In ordinary conditions, every part of the device will form B-DNA and the two DX molecules will both be on the same side of the shaft's axis. When cobalt hexammine is added to the solution, the central part of the shaft converts to Z-DNA and one DX molecule rotates about 3.5 turns relative to the other; the odd half-turn means that they are now on opposite sides of the shaft's axis. Removal of the cobalt hexammine reverts the device back to its original structure. We demonstrated that the motion was taking place by using spectroscopy involving two colored dyes attached to the DX molecules.

This B-Z device is quite robust, but it suffers from a flaw. Were a bunch of different B-Z devices incorporated into a larger superstructure (for example, one of the two-dimensional lattices discussed earlier), the entire structure would have only two states: every machine in the B state or every one in the Z state. To control a collection of machines individually requires devices with independent triggers. With DNA, of course, there is a natural way to do this, by using DNA strands as the triggers and having a different base sequence trigger each machine.

To implement this scheme, Hao Yan, now at Duke, Xiaoping Zhang of New York University, Shen and I devised a system that changes shape when different strands bind to it. The system consists of two parallel DNA double helices that each reduce to a single strand in a central crossover region. The crossover region can assume two different states according to which particular strands have been added to the solution to bind to the single-strand sections. The two states of the device are called PX ("paranemic crossover") and JX ("juxta-posed"). When the device is in the PX state, the two helices on one side of the central junction are rotated about a half-turn from their positions in the JX state.

Adding a particular pair of strands (called set strands) to the solution puts the device in the JX state by binding to the central region without crossing over. To change to the PX state, we must first remove these set strands. In 2000 Bernard Yurke and his colleagues at Lucent Technologies showed that a strand can be extracted from DNA by binding the strand's full complement to it. To implement this process, our set strands have short ends that remain unpaired with the machine. When we add a full complementary strand to the solution, it begins by joining to the unpaired extension and then strips off the rest of the set strand from the device.

With the first set strands removed from the frame, we can then add different set strands, which bind to the central region and cross over there. That binding turns the two double helices and puts the device in the PX state. The process can be reversed by removing the second set strands and adding back the first ones. In this way, the double helices can be turned back and forth at will. A number of different PX-JX devices can be operated independently by adding and removing set strands designed for their individual binding regions.

We used atomic-force microscopy to verify how our device moved. We made a long chain of these devices and connected a large trapezoid-shape DNA unit to one side of each device. When all the devices are in the PX state, the trapezoids lie on the same side of the chain. When all are in the JX state, the trapezoids alternate sides, in a zigzag pattern.

In 2000 Yurke and his colleagues demonstrated nanoscopic "tweezers" made of three strands of DNA. Set strands, which Yurke calls fuel strands, opened and closed the tweezers. Other researchers have used similar methods to switch on the activity of ribozymes—enzymes made of RNA. In 1998 Michael P. Robinson and Andrew D. Ellington of the University of Texas at Austin demonstrated a 10,000-fold enhancement of a ribozyme's activity by the addition of an appropriate set strand, which bound to the ribozyme, changing its conformation.

## The Future

A crucial goal for nanotechnology based on DNA is to extend the successes in two dimensions to three dimensions. When that has been accomplished, we will have demonstrated the ability to design solid materials by specifying a series of DNA sequences and then combining them. If the systems are highly ordered, then the crystallographic experiments involving molecules held within a regularly repeating framework mentioned earlier will be feasible.

Another goal is to incorporate DNA devices within the frameworks. This accomplishment would be the first step toward nanorobotics involving complex motions and a diversity of structural states, which would enable us to build chemical assembly lines. Using devices similar to the ones described here, we could assemble new materials with high precision. As a prototype, James W. Canary and Philip S. Lukeman of N.Y.U., Lei Zhu, now at the University of Texas at Austin, and I recently assembled a small piece of nylon on a nucleic acid backbone. Someday we expect to be able to make new polymers with specific properties and topologies (such as windings of their backbones).

Achieving these goals primarily entails the use of DNA as a programmable component, but neither crystallography nor nanoelectronics can rely on DNA alone. For instance, nanoelectronic components, such as metallic nanoparticles or carbon nanotubes, will have to be combined with DNA molecules in systems and liquid solutions that are compatible with both the DNA and the other components. Given the diverse chemical nature of these molecules, achieving this will not be simple. In addition, even if the nanoelectronics can be constructed by DNA self-assembly, the nanomachines ultimately need to interact with the macroscopic world in a manner that is more sophisticated than the addition and removal of set strands from a solution. This challenge is likely to be formidable.

A nanotechnological dream machine is one that can replicate. Unlike linear DNA, however, branched DNA does not lend itself readily to self-replication. Yet late last year William M. Shih, Joel D. Quispe and Gerald F. Joyce of the Scripps Research Institute in La Jolla, Calif., took an exciting first step toward self-replicating DNA objects. They built an octahedron from one long strand of DNA (about 1,700 bases), using five short "helper" strands to complete the assembly. Each edge of the octahedron is made of two interlinked DNA double helices—a series of DX and PX molecules. The edges were each about 14 nanometers long, or about four turns of a double helix. A folded octahedron cannot reproduce, but in the unfolded state, the long strand is readily cloned millions of times by a standard biotechnology process called PCR (polymerase chain reaction). It is still a far cry from the replication achieved by every living organism, but by the time the Watson-Crick centenary comes around, we should have DNA-based machines that do as well.

## More to Explore

A DNA-Fuelled Molecular Machine Made of DNA. Bernard Yurke, Andrew J. Turberfield, Allen P. Mills, Jr., Friedrich C. Simmel and Jennifer L. Neumann in *Nature*, Vol. 406, pages 605–608; August 10, 2000.

Logical Computation Using Algorithmic Self-Assembly of DNA Triple Crossover Molecules. Chengde Mao, Thomas H. LaBean, John H. Reif and Nadrian C. Seeman in *Nature*, Vol. 407, pages 493–496; September 28, 2000. (Erratum: *Nature*, Vol. 408, page 750; December 7, 2000.)

A Robust DNA Mechanical Device Controlled by Hybridization Topology. Hao Yan, Xiaoping Zhang, Zhiyong Shen and Nadrian C. Seeman in *Nature*, Vol. 415, pages 62–65; January 3, 2002.

DNA in a Material World. Nadrian C. Seeman in *Nature*, Vol. 421, pages 427–431; January 23, 2003.

DNA as an Engineering Material. Andrew Turberfield in *Physics World*, Vol. 16, No. 3, pages 43–46; March 2003.

A 1.7-Kilobase Single-Stranded DNA That Folds into a Nanoscale Octahedron. William M. Shih, Joel D. Quispe and Gerald F. Joyce in *Nature*, Vol. 427, pages 618–621; February 12, 2004.

Nadrian C. Seeman's laboratory Web site: **http:// seemanlab4.chem.nyu.edu/**

## The Author

*NADRIAN C. ("NED") SEEMAN* trained in crystallography, but his frustrations with a macromolecular crystallization experiment led him to the idea that DNA junctions could be used in a new approach to crystallization. Ever since then, he has been trying to implement this concept and its spin-offs. For the past 16 years, Seeman has worked in the department of chemistry at New York University. When told in the mid-1980s that what he was doing was nanotechnology, his response was similar to that of M. Jourdain, the title character of Molière's *Bourgeois Gentilhomme*, who was delighted to discover that he had been speaking prose all his life.

# "Nanotubes in
# 6. the Clean Room"

by Gary Stix

*Talismans of a thousand graduate projects may*
*soon make their way into electronic memories*

Charles M. Lieber, a major figure in nanotechnology, asked one of his graduate students in 1998 to undertake the design of a radically new type of computer memory. It would read and write digital bits with memory elements that measured less than 10 billionths of a meter (10 nanometers). Until then, the student, a German native named Thomas Rueckes, had been spending his time in Lieber's laboratory at Harvard University measuring the electrical and material properties of carbon nanotubes. These cylinders, measuring but a nanometer or so in diameter, display a surface of hexagonal carbon rings that give the material the appearance of a honeycomb or chicken wire. Since the discovery of nanotubes in 1991, the scientific community has lauded them for their superlative material and electrical properties.

Lieber wanted to know whether Rueckes could come up with a concept involving nanotubes that could be submitted for funding under a molecular electronics program funded by the Defense Advanced Research Projects Agency. Rueckes pored over books and review articles for a few days, but nothing good suggested itself. One evening he left the chemistry lab and crossed the street to the cafeteria at the Harvard Science Center. On his pizza run, he passed the Harvard Mark 1, the 55-foot-long monstrosity, a predecessor of modern computers, that had served the U.S. Navy as a calculator for gunnery and ballistic computations until 1959. It now decorated the center's hallway. Back in the lab, he remembered that the Mark 1 operated by moving mechanical relays from one position to another. "That is what flipped a switch in my brain," he remembers. "I could see a picture of how to build a memory."

Many researchers were trying to use nanotubes as wires or components in new transistor designs. The Mark 1 inspiration prompted Rueckes to focus instead on their extraordinary tensile strength and resilience. Nanotubes, he imagined, might flex up and down to represent a 0 and a 1 state, like hyper-shrunken versions of the relays in the Mark 1. "We sat down and worked out a proposal in a couple of days and submitted it to DARPA, and they funded it in one day," Rueckes says.

Until his graduation in 2001, Rueckes continued to develop the concept. As he worked, he realized that nanotubes had more and more to offer. They could, in theory, provide the makings of a universal memory, one that combined the speed of static random-access memory, the low cost of dynamic random-access memory (DRAM), and the nonvolatility (instant-on operation) of flash memory. Its status as *uber*-material would also make it a low consumer of electrical power as well as resistant to potentially damaging heat, cold and magnetism.

## When Billionths Meet Trillions

On paper, the design was relatively simple. Nanotubes would serve as individually addressable electromechanical switches arrayed across the surface of a microchip, storing hundreds of gigabits of information, maybe even a terabit. An electric field applied to a nanotube would cause it to flex downward into a depression etched onto the chip's surface, where it would contact another nanotube (in current designs, it touches a metal electrode). Once bent, the nanotubes could remain that way, including when the power was turned off, allowing for nonvolatile operation. Van der Waals forces, which are weak molecular attractions, would hold the switch in place until application of a field of different polarity caused the nanotube to return to its straightened position.

Even before Rueckes had finished at Harvard, he received a visit from an executive at an Internet company who was looking to strike out in a new direction. Greg Schmergel, a Harvard M.B.A. and former management consultant, had come to learn through his experience as an Internet entrepreneur about the fickleness of the new medium and how low the barriers for new entrants were. His company, a successful venture called ExpertCentral.com, which provided professional services references, had experienced these vicissitudes firsthand. It was scooped up by About.com, which, in turn, was bought by Primedia.

Nanotechnology seemed less amenable to dot-com-style feeding frenzies. Most people, even scientists, could not offer a cogent definition, except to point to the science-fiction section at Barnes & Noble. Schmergel did not know all that much about it either, although it did seem as faraway from an Internet company as anything he could imagine. But Schmergel, who was also heir to a long tradition of entrepreneurship (his father started one of the first

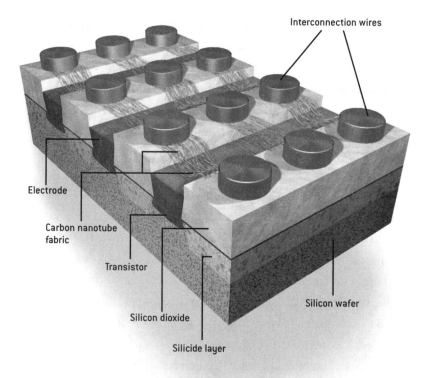

Arrays of carbon nanotubes, called fabrics, constitute the 0 and 1 switching elements for an innovative memory chip designed by Nantero, a section of which is shown here.

biotech companies), did know business, whereas Rueckes understood, as well as anyone could, the emerging field of nanotechnology.

So, in 2001, Schmergel and Rueckes, along with Brent M. Segal, another former Harvard chemistry doctoral student, formed Nantero, a name whose genesis again combined the small ("nano") and the large ("tero," a corruption of "tera," or trillions, as in trillions of bits). Lieber himself opted to pursue more advanced projects in his Harvard lab, smart nanowires that would assemble on their own into finished devices and that might use biological or other unorthodox signals for communication among device structures.

The immediate mandate for Nantero was to move beyond an advanced graduate project to create a device that could be manufactured in a working semiconductor facility. The company set up shop in a Woburn, Mass., industrial park populated largely by biotechnology firms. Schmergel tried to remove as many distractions as possible for his researchers: Nantero is still not listed in the Woburn telephone directory. Early on the team approached a number of big chip manufacturers. Engineers there did not always greet their presentations warmly. Rueckes recalls how one manager sputtered: "We don't want your virus in our plant."

## Ironing Things Out

Nanotubes, purchased from bulk suppliers, are a form of high-tech soot that contains a residue that averages

5 percent iron, a contaminant whose very mention
can produce involuntary tremors in managers of
multimillion-dollar clean rooms. The Nantero team
devoted much of its early development to devising a
complex filtration process to reduce the amount of
iron to the parts-per-billion level.

Adapting rolled-carbon chicken wire to the standard
photolithography and etching process that patterns and
removes material to form electrical circuitry proved
just as daunting. New chip factories cost more than
$2 billion, and notoriously conservative plant managers
had no inclination to retool to integrate nanotubes
into the standard CMOS (complementary metal oxide
semiconductor) manufacturing process. When Nantero
started, no good options existed for forming a nanotube on the surface of a wafer (the round silicon disk
from which chips are carved) without interfering with
adjoining electrical circuitry. Deposition of nanotubes onto the wafer using a gas vapor required
temperatures so high that the circuitry already in place
would be ruined. Alternatively, coating the wafer with a
nanotube-containing solvent by spinning the disk like
a phonograph record also had its problems. A suitable
solvent, chlorobenzene, was considered excessively
toxic and had been banned from chip factories.

Nantero devised a proprietary solvent suitable for
spin coating. The thin film of nanotubes left after the
solvent is removed can be subjected to lithography and
etching that leaves the surface of the wafer with evenly
spaced groupings of nanotubes. On close inspection,
the conglomeration of threadlike nanotubes resembles a

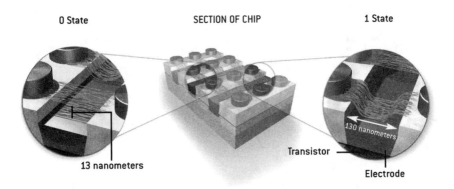

0 State SECTION OF CHIP 1 State

13 nanometers

130 nanometers

Transistor

Electrode

Sagging and straightening represent the 1 and 0 states for a random-access memory made up of groupings of nanotubes. In its 0 state, the fabric remains suspended above the electrode (*left*). When a transistor turns on, the electrode produces an electric field that causes a nanotube fabric to bend and touch an electrode, a configuration that denotes a 1 state (*right*).

helter-skelter unwoven fabric. An electric field applied to one of the fabric elements bends it downward until it contacts an electrode, a position that represents a digital 1. ASML, a major semiconductor tool manufacturer, helped to refine this process with Nantero.

When Nantero had gained confidence with the technology, it began a new round of visits to semiconductor manufacturers. In 2003 LSI Logic, a leading maker of customized chips for the telecommunications, storage and consumer electronics industries, agreed to bring the process for making what Nantero calls nanotube random-access memory (NRAM) into its factory in Gresham, Ore. To everyone's surprise, the collaborators had a working prototype within nine months. The project was quickly put on an early-development track,

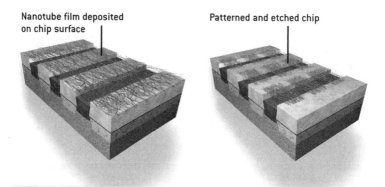

**Nanotube film deposited on chip surface**

**Patterned and etched chip**

Layer of nanotubes gets deposited onto a section of the chip's surface (*left*) before material is removed (*right*) using standard semiconductor lithography and etching. Further processing steps (*not shown*) are needed to complete fabrication of the chip.

targeting the first commercial production memories for 2006. "I'm still amazed that the darn things work, because I was a little skeptical," says Norm Armour, general manager for the Gresham plant. LSI is interested in pursuing the technology as a replacement for fast-access memory modules (static RAM) embedded on microprocessors that consume an ever larger part of the chip area. A nanotube memory could be faster and much smaller while consuming less power.

In coming months, LSI and Nantero will strive to increase "yield," the ability to make millions of nanotube memories with near-perfect repeatability. To achieve high yields, engineers must attend to a multitude of details. If, for instance, the cavity over which the nanotube is suspended does not form sharp enough edges, it can adversely affect the device's electrical characteristics, changing the voltage at which it turns on and off. "The yield question is a big question, but we don't see anything insurmountable," comments Verne Hornback, LSI's senior project manager on the Nantero collaboration.

Although nanotube memories have intrigued the industry, skepticism remains. "Nantero has a great idea, but I believe it is a long way from having a credible manufacturing process," says G. Dan Hutcheson, who heads the market analysis firm VLSI Research in Santa Clara, Calif. He adds: "I will be very surprised if Nantero can make a scaled-up device that can compete cost-effectively with a DRAM as they claim, because I doubt that their process is scalable and repeatable. So the yields will be low."

A leader in this area of research, IBM has not pursued nanotube memories. The company has decided to focus on using nanotubes to replace a critical component that shuttles electrons from one side of a transistor to another. "We have no problems in finding choices for memory, but we're running out of choices for logic. And nanotubes offer unique properties for logic," observes Phaedon Avouris, a scientist at the IBM Thomas J. Watson Research Center.

Of course, Nantero thinks that the development work with LSI this year will disprove the doomsayers— for instance, the use of nanotube fabrics instead of the individual nanotubes as switching elements, which was an approach employed in the early design at Harvard, mitigates concerns about variability in size among the tubes. And the company has already attracted another partner, BAE Systems, to work on defense and aerospace applications for the radiation-resistant NRAMs. Even if the chips do not meet expectations, Nantero, which has filed for 60 patents and been granted 10 of those applications, will be left with valuable manufacturing know-how that could be licensed to others who want to combine nanotubes with chipmaking.

Just getting nanotubes into a factory at all marks a milestone. "The biggest victory we've had is to bring the process into a standard CMOS facility," LSI's Hornback remarks. A nanotube chip in a cell phone would be sweet vindication for the legions of researchers who have spent the early part of their careers poking and shocking these invisible specks. Until now, virtually the only products that incorporate this material that is stronger than steel and as hard as diamond have been glowing press releases from universities and industry.

## More to Explore

**The Incredible Shrinking Circuit.** Charles M. Lieber in *Scientific American*, Vol. 285, No. 3, pages 58–64; September 2001.

**Supertubes.** Phaedon Avouris in *IEEE Spectrum*, Vol. 41, No. 8, pages 40–45; August 2004.

Information about Nantero and NRAMs can be accessed at **www.nantero.com**

# "Crossbar
# 7. Nanocomputers"

by Philip J. Kuekes, Gregory S. Snider,
and R. Stanley Williams

*Crisscrossing assemblies of defect-prone nanowires
could succeed today's silicon-based circuits*

In a little over half a century, the number of transistors
on a silicon chip has grown from just one to nearly a
billion—an accomplishment celebrated as Moore's
Law. By greatly enhancing digital machines' ability to
crunch numbers, execute logical operations and store
data, this unprecedented manufacturing success has
enabled revolutionary changes in our day-to-day lives
while spawning one of the planet's largest and most
influential industries.

As more and more transistors are packed onto
silicon integrated circuits (ICs) during the next decade
and a half, the lengths of the smallest chip features will
shrink to nearly the molecular scale. Even the most
optimistic proponents of ICs believe that major innovations will be required to reach the ultimate operating
limit of the silicon transistor: a length for functional
features around 10 nanometers (nm), or about 30 atoms
long. Finding alternative technologies that can further
shrink computing devices is crucial to maintaining
technological progress. But because of the silicon IC's
amazingly successful track record, the performance
bar for any successor is so high it will take at least a

decade to develop candidates that will be available when they are needed.

Researchers worldwide are exploring several exciting alternatives. Quantum computing, for instance, is a novel technique that takes advantage of "spooky" quantum-mechanical properties to process information. Quantum computing is, however, decades away from realization, and even then it remains unclear how useful it would be for most applications. Many research groups are therefore searching for a midterm alternative that could be ready for commercialization in about 10 years. To be economically viable, such a technology must share a great deal with the existing IC processor infrastructure, including critical items like fabrication foundries and software platforms.

Our research team at Hewlett-Packard (HP) Laboratories views the crossbar architecture as the most likely path forward. A crossbar consists of one set of parallel nanowires (less than 100 atoms wide) that cross over a second set. A material that can be stimulated electrically to conduct either more electricity or less is sandwiched between the two

## Overview/Nanoelectronics

- Moving beyond today's silicon integrated chip technology will require shrinking logic and memory circuits to the scale of a few nanometers. Large arrays of intersecting nanowires called crossbars provide the basis for one of the best candidate technologies for nanocomputing success.
- The nanowires that comprise crossbars are so small that atomic defects and flaws in their manufacture are unavoidable and serious. Building redundancy into the circuitry and using coding theory techniques compensate for the many imperfections.

sets of wires. The resulting interwire junctions form a switch at each intersection between crossing wires that can hold its "on" or "off" status over time.

Crossbars offer several benefits: The regular pattern of crisscrossing nanowires makes manufacturing relatively straightforward, especially compared with the complex structures of microprocessors. Its arraylike composition provides clear ways to instill defect tolerance in circuits. The structure can be built using a wide range of substances and processes, which provides tremendous flexibility in adapting existing designs to new materials. Finally, this single geometry can provide memory, logic and interconnection, making it very adaptable.

## (Criss)crossing Over

Our team's journey toward this avenue of research began in 1995, when one of us (Williams) moved to HP from the chemistry department at the University of California, Los Angeles. Though not a computer expert, he did know a few things about electronics: one, that a computer's circuits had to be perfect to operate correctly and, two, that random atomic fluctuations at room temperature and above (caused by entropy) would make it impossible to build a perfect machine from billions of components, each composed of only a few atoms. Even atomic-scale irregularities impose significant variations on the size of nanodevices, which can destroy their electrical properties. Consequently, some

## Build Top-Down or Bottom-Up?

The field of nanoscale fabrication is extremely active today, with many competing techniques under study. These approaches can be classified into two categories: top-down and bottom-up. The former examples resemble conventional IC manufacturing methods that use photolithography followed by chemical etching or deposition of materials to create the desired features. The latter approaches are based on extensions of chemical or biochemical processes by which atoms or molecules self-assemble into a desired configuration because of their planned, inherent properties. Most investigators in this field agree that some combination of the two approaches will be required to build future nanoscale circuits.

At HP, our team uses imprint lithography to create the crossbars. We and our collaborators employ electron beam lithography to construct molds for the circuits. Although this process is slow and costly, we can make duplicates of the final product, which then are used to stamp out large quantities of circuits, much as vinyl LP records were made.

A thin layer of a polymer or polymer precursor coats a substrate, the mold is pressed into this soft layer, and the impressed pattern hardens under exposure to heat or ultraviolet light. The advantage of this approach is that electron-beam lithography can fabricate arbitrary wire geometries on the mold. The drawback is that the present resolution of the features in a set of parallel wires is limited to roughly 30-nanometer half-pitch (half the distance between the centers of two wires, a standard industry measure), although we are working on a number of techniques to improve on this performance. —P.J.K., G.S.S. and R.S.W.

sizable fraction of the tiny devices will not work. It was natural for Williams to conclude that nanoelectronics were therefore impossible and that his research at HP should focus on other technologies.

A chance meeting the following year with an HP computer architect (Kuekes) changed that perception dramatically and set the pair on an unexpected path. Kuekes told Williams about a supercomputer called Teramac that he and others (including Snider) had built. Teramac operated perfectly, even though about 220,000 of its components (approximately 3 percent of the total) were defective. The trick, Kuekes said, was that the supercomputer's design had significant redundancy in its interconnect circuitry. After all the flaws were located and catalogued, programs run on the computer were compiled to avoid the broken parts, essentially by routing around the defects via the extra connections.

Williams saw at once that Teramac's tolerance of defects provided a way to construct computers that operate perfectly despite huge numbers of "broken" nanoscale parts. That summer Williams and visiting U.C.L.A. chemist James R. Heath worked on applying the concepts of nanoparticle assembly (assembling complex structures out of tiny building blocks) to computers. After much discussion with Kuekes and Snider about the defect tolerance of chemically assembled computing systems, Williams and Heath wrote a paper about the topic as an educational exercise. To the surprise of all involved, it was taken seriously and eventually published in *Science* in 1998.

## Rapid Results Required

That same year Bruce E. Gnade and William L. Warren, then program directors at the Defense Advanced Research Projects Agency (DARPA), recognized that effective architecture was critical for developing the new nanoscale device technologies the agency was supporting. At the time, interest in molecular electronics was enjoying a resurgence, years after it had first been proposed in 1974 by Avi Aviram of IBM and Mark A. Ratner of Northwestern University. It was not, however, until the early 1990s that Mark A. Reed of Yale University and James M. Tour of Rice University actually started measuring the electrical properties and synthesizing new molecules for electronics. Gnade and Warren understood that electronic devices without an architecture to link them into a useful circuit were mere intellectual curiosities. Their challenge to the research community to define a workable architecture for molecular devices kick-started the research efforts of many groups and encouraged the formation of several significant collaborations.

Our HP/U.C.L.A. team immediately embraced that challenge, but we faced a dilemma. The Teramac-inspired architecture that we had proposed would have required five years to develop, but DARPA wanted tangible results (as a 16-bit memory device) in only two. Heath, Kuekes and Williams brainstormed during the next several weeks to come up with a concept that could meet the deadline. Kuekes and Williams were aware of HP's magnetic random-access memory project and understood that the simple crossbar structure on which it was based was the ultimate abstraction of the Teramac configuration.

Heath pointed out that a crossbar "looked like a crystal" and that it should therefore be possible to build such a system chemically. What was needed was some way to connect each pair of intersecting wires in the crossbar with a switch that could be turned on and off at will. Williams suggested that an electrochemically active material sandwiched between the wires should make it possible to change the electrical resistance of the contacts substantially and reversibly, by applying the appropriate voltages across the two nanowires. That is, the switch would be closed by electrochemically shrinking the quantum-mechanical "tunneling" gap that the electrons have to jump across to get from one electrode to the other. Applying the opposite voltage bias to widen the tunneling gap and raise the electrical resistance would reopen the switch.

Heath provided the material we needed. He introduced our collaboration to molecules that had been designed by J. Fraser Stoddart, then a new U.C.L.A. faculty member, to operate as electrochemically actuated mechanical switches. The concept was that anything that will change shape between two wires should also affect the ability of electrons to tunnel from one wire to another. A key step was persuading a very busy Stoddart to chemically modify his molecules, which he had christened rotaxanes, to make them oily. This alteration enabled Heath to place a small drop of rotaxanes on a water surface so they would spread out to form a film one molecule thick, which was transferred onto a substrate (a process called the Langmuir-Blodgett technique) on which the bottom set of wires had been formed. After that, we deposited the top set of wires by evaporating metal through a mask, which completed the circuit. These early experiments led to several

U.S. patent applications, a proposal to DARPA and
another paper in *Science.*

## Making the Cut

Despite considerable skepticism on the part of the
research community, our crossbar and electrochemical
switch concept was accepted by DARPA for its two-year
trial, along with several others. Early in this effort the
Heath and Stoddart research groups demonstrated that
rotaxane molecules sandwiched between electrodes
could indeed toggle between high- and low-resistance
states. We and others, including Charles Lieber's group
at Harvard University as well as the Reed and Tour
groups, have since seen a range of different nanoscale
switching mechanisms. The diverse observations and
approaches generated some confusion within the
broader research community, and the various switching
phenomena have yet to be sorted out, but the existence
of electrical switching is today widely recognized.
Dozens of research teams across the globe are now
working to develop robust nanoscale electrical switches
based on atoms or molecules [*see box on page 126*].

Using the crossbar structure, our U.C.L.A. partners
became the first group to demonstrate a working 16-bit
memory for the DARPA program in 2000. Their success
encouraged the agency to fund a successor program
with a far more ambitious goal: the fabrication of a
16-kilobit memory with a density of 100 billion bits per
square centimeter. This objective sets the bar extremely

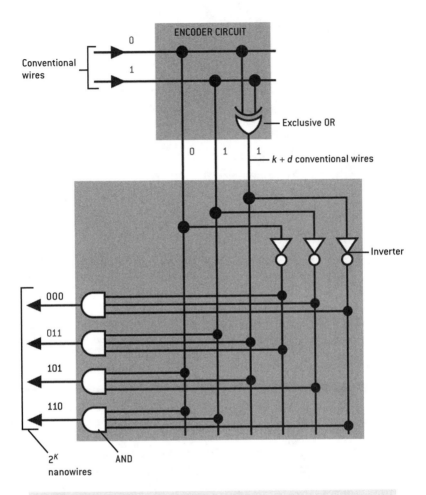

DEMULTIPLEXER enables conventional wires on silicon chips to control a far greater number of nanowires. If k is the number of conventional wires, the multiplexer can control $2^k$ nanowires. An additional d conventional wires provide sufficient redundancy for the control to work despite broken connections between nanowires and conventional wires. In this simplified diagram, k = 2 and d = 1; two micron-scale wires control four nanowires with one bit of redundancy . In this example, the conventional wires input the switch address 01 (gray), to which the encoder circuit adds a redundant bit, yielding the coded address 011. The coded address then activates the nanowire in the demultiplexer designated 011.

high, because it requires fabrication capabilities that are not expected to become available to the semiconductor industry until around 2018.

Our group at HP continues to invent new types of circuits based on the crossbar—notably, defect-tolerant memories and different families of logic circuits. Interesting modifications of the original architectural concept also have been developed by André DeHon of the California Institute of Technology, who collaborates with the Lieber group, and Konstantin K. Likharev of Stony Brook University. Although the crossbar and switch architecture started off as the dark-horse candidate in the DARPA challenge, it has now been adopted and adapted by many research groups worldwide, including those of Masakazu Aono of the National Institute for Materials Science in Japan and Rainer Waser of the Research Center Jülich in Germany.

To understand the crossbar approach, we must discuss the nature of the switch and crossbar structure, the fabrication of crossbars from nanoscale wires [*see box on page 116*] and the possibility of building reliable circuits from unreliable components.

## From Micro to Nano and Back

The philosophy behind the nanoscale crossbar is that we must learn to live with its unavoidable imperfections and work around them. The "find and avoid" strategy of Teramac will work as long as it is possible to communicate with the nanowires. This, however, poses another question: How does one bridge the gaps in size and number of wires between nanoelectronics and the conventional-scale silicon ICs that will be required to control the crossbars? If only one-to-one connections can be made, nanoscale crossbars would afford no net advantage. We can solve that problem by making the electrical connections through a demultiplexer, a sub-circuit that takes as an input a binary number (such as 1010) and selects a single nanowire that has that binary string as a unique identifier [*see illustration on page 121*]. In our case, the demultiplexer is a special type of crossbar in which many nanowires connect to a small number of conventional wires.

The number of wires required to input a binary address is the same as the length of the digital names, but the quantity of nanowires that can be addressed equals the number of unique addresses. For example, a string four bits long (0000, 0001, 0010 and so on) can specify 16 unique addresses. Therefore, four micron-scale wires can control 16 nanowires. This fact is important because, to make building the nanoscale circuits worthwhile, one needs to be able to control a lot of nanocircuitry with little conventional electronics. In general, if $k$ is the number of conventional wires feeding into the demultiplexer, it can individually control $2^k$ nanowires, which is very favorable exponential scaling.

A big problem occurs, however, if one of the connections between a nanowire in the demultiplexer and a conventional wire is broken. Then it is no longer possible to distinguish among the $k$ different nanowires that share that defective bit in its address. (For instance, if the last bit in the string is broken, then 0000 and 0001 seem identical, as do 1110 and 1111 and other pairs.) Hence, one bad connection in the demultiplexer leads to the loss of all the nanocircuitry that is downstream from $k$ nanowires—a catastrophic failure. This result appears to require that demultiplexers, which are half nanocircuitry, be perfect—a violation of our guiding principle that nanoelectronics will be defective.

We find the solution to this quandary in the field of coding theory, which engineers apply when transmitting digital information through noisy environments (as in orbital satellite communications). The general idea is: first, break up a message into blocks of binary data—strings of 0s and 1s. Each block is then extended by adding some extra bits to make a larger block, the code. The extra bits are calculated with an algebraic expression utilizing the bits in the original message block as inputs. When this larger message is sent through the air or some other noisy environment, a few of the bits in the coded message may be garbled (some 1s are turned into 0s and vice versa). By running the code backward on the receiving end, however, the original message can be recovered exactly (as long as the number of flipped bits does not overwhelm the code).

With the guidance of Gadiel Seroussi, Ronnie Roth and Warren Robinett of HP, our team has applied this concept to protect our nanowires from broken connections in the demultiplexer. Rather than numbering the nanowires consecutively, we use an extended address space in which the number of wires entering the demultiplexer is larger than the minimum number needed to specify each nanowire uniquely (by an additional $d$ wires). In this case, it turns out that each nanowire can have several broken connections to the conventional wires, yet the demultiplexer can still successfully address all the nanowires. The degree of redundancy required depends on the probability of connection defects; a relatively small amount of redundancy (about 40 percent) can improve the effective manufacturing yield of a demultiplexer from 0.0001 to 0.9999 if the defect rate of the connections in the demultiplexer is 0.01.

## Making Memories

Since that first 16-bit memory device, both the Heath group and our team at HP have demonstrated 64-bit memories at 62-nm half-pitch (which is half the distance between the centers of two adjacent wires, a standard semiconductor industry measure) in 2002 and last year a one-kilobit crossbar at 30-nm half-pitch, using different approaches for the wires and switches. (In comparison, the half-pitch of the most advanced semiconductor IC in 2005 is 90 nm.) Each nanowire in these demonstration memories was connected to an individual contact. We wrote a bit as a 1 (low-resistance) or a 0 (high-resistance) simply by applying

## Groups Researching Crossbar Architectures

| GROUP(S) | INSTITUTION(S) | SWITCH |
|---|---|---|
| J. R. Heath/ J. F. Stoddart | Caltech/U.C.L.A. | Rotaxane monolayer between silicon and titanium nanowires |
| C. Lieber/ A. DeHon | Harvard University/ Caltech | Silicon nanowire field-effect transistors |
| M. Aono | National Institute for Materials Science, Japan | Silver sulfide ionic conductor (silver-based atomic switch) |
| R. Waser | Research Center Jülich, Germany | Defect motion in ferroelectric thin films |
| K. K. Likharev | Stony Brook University | Molecular single-electron transistor |
| Quantum Science Research | Hewlett-Packard Laboratories | Metal nanowire oxidation/reduction |

a bias voltage that exceeded the threshold for directly toggling the desired switch across its two wires. As long as the voltage threshold for recording a 1 or a 0 is relatively sharp and the variation in "write" voltages among the junctions in the array is less than one half the switching voltage, this procedure ensures that only the desired bit in the array is written (and no others are accidentally written or erased). We read the bit stored in the switch by applying a much lower voltage across the selected crossing wires and measuring the resistance at their junction. These initial results proved promising—in HP's 64-bit memory, the resistance ratio between 1 ("on") and 0 ("off") exceeded 100, making the bits very easy to read.

With the goal of nanoscale memory within reach (the DARPA challenge requires a half-pitch of 16 nm), our next big hurdle is to perform universal computation with nanoscale logic circuits. With Duncan R. Stewart at HP, we have configured crossbars to perform simple logic (Boolean AND and OR operations) by setting the resistance values of switches in a crossbar. The range of logic that can be performed, however, is limited without the NOT operation, or signal inversion, which changes a 1 to a 0 and a 0 to a 1. The wired logic functions also necessarily cause the voltage levels to trail off; if one tries to use too many in a series circuit, 1s and 0s would no longer be distinguishable and computation would not be possible.

In silicon ICs, transistors perform both signal restoration and inversion. This fact has motivated the Heath and Lieber groups to fabricate transistors made from silicon nanowires. We and DeHon have described logic circuits with a "tile and mosaic" topology that can be built using transistors and other elements that are fabricated into a crossbar. Because this approach employs current IC technology, however, eventually it suffers from the aforementioned limitations, so it does not offer an extension beyond Moore's Law. As an alternative, we are investigating signal inversion and restoration without transistors.

Our team is building an unusual form of crossbar logic circuit with arrays of switches and wired ANDs and ORs. In this case, the switches perform a latching operation, which we recently demonstrated with Stewart. We define the voltage level needed to turn a switch on as a 1 and that to turn it off as a 0. Any wire connected to the input of a switch will perforce set that switch to the wire's present logical state, thus transferring one bit of information from "logic" to "memory."

Once stored as a memory state, that bit can be employed in further logic operations by connecting the output wire from the switch to a voltage supply (in our case, a wire from the clock that controls the timing of the operations). This new connection can then be used to restore the voltage of the logic state to its desired value when it has degraded. Another trick is to switch the voltages representing a 1 and a 0 on the output wires, which inverts the logic signal. This change supplies the logical NOT operation and, combined with either ANDs or ORs, is sufficient to perform any computation. Hence, we managed to create the signal restoration and inversion functions without the use of transistors or their semiconductor properties in a crossbar logic circuit.

## Beyond Silicon ICs

The path to universal computing beyond transistor integrated circuits is still highly uncertain, but the crossbar architecture has emerged during the past several years as a principal contender for a new computing paradigm. Much remains to be done. Three different areas of research must advance rapidly and together: architecture, device physics and nanomanufacturing. Ensuring good communications across disciplinary boundaries will be as challenging as solving the technical issues. Success will require multiple teams of researchers who are simultaneously competing against and cooperating with one another, such as the participants in the DARPA challenge.

Defect tolerance will be a necessary element of any future strategy for nanoelectronics. The crossbar architecture is ideal for implementing strategies based on finding and avoiding bad components and on coding theory to compensate for mistakes. Future circuits may actually be more robust than current electronics, even though they will start out with a high fraction of defective components. The built-in redundancy will make them resistant to forces (such as radiation exposure) that cause catastrophic failures in conventional circuits and instead enable their performance to degrade gracefully.

The quantum-mechanical nature of tunneling switches is suited for nanoscale circuits. As the feature sizes of devices shrink, the electrons in them behave more like quantum-mechanical bodies. Such switches should be able to scale down to nearly single-atom dimensions—which suggests just how far the future miniaturization of electronic circuitry might someday go.

## More to Explore

**Configurable Computing.** John Villasenor and
William H. Mangione-Smith in *Scientific American*,
Vol. 276, No. 6, pages 66–71; June 1997.

**A Defect-Tolerant Computer Architecture:
Opportunities for Nanotechnology.** J. R. Heath,
P. J. Kuekes, G. S. Snider and R. S. Williams in
*Science*, Vol. 280, pages 1716–1721; June 1998.

**Computing with Molecules.** Mark A. Reed and James
M. Tour in *Scientific American*, Vol. 282, No. 6,
pages 86–93; June 2000.

**Feynman Lectures in Computation.** Paperbound edition.
Richard P. Feynman. Edited by Tony Hey and
Robin W. Allen. Perseus Books Group, 2000.

The International Technology Roadmap for
Semiconductors (ITRS) Web site is at **http://
public.itrs.net/**

## The Authors

*PHILIP J. KUEKES, GREGORY S. SNIDRE* and
*R. STANLEY WILLIAMS* develop next-generation computing technologies at the Quantum Science Research
(QSR) program at Hewlett-Packard Laboratories in
Palo Alto, Calif. Kuekes devises novel ideas in the areas
of computation, electronic circuits and devices, and
quantum information research. The chief architect of
the QSR program has designed and built leading-edge
computers for more than 30 years. Snider, currently a

consultant with HP, is exploring ways to improve the architectural design of nanoelectronics. He has worked previously on logic circuit design, compilers, operating systems, logic synthesis, digital signal processing, computer security and networking systems. Williams, as HP Senior Fellow and director of HP's QSR program, guides the multidisciplinary team that designs, builds and tests new nanocircuits. In the past Williams focused on solid-state chemistry and physics, but his primary interest now is the study of the intersection of nanoscience and information technology.

# Web Sites

Due to the changing nature of Internet links, Rosen Publishing has developed an online list of Web sites related to the subject of this book. This site is updated regularly. Please use this link to access the list:

http://www.rosenlinks.com/saces/nano

# For Further Reading

Booker, Richard. *Nanotechnology for Dummies.* Hoboken, NJ: Wiley, 2005.

Foster, Lynn E. *Nanotechnology: Science, Innovation and Opportunity.* Upper Saddle River, NJ: Prentice Hall, 2005.

Fritz, Sandy. *Nanotechnology: Invisible Machines.* North Mankato, MN: Smart Apple Media, 2003.

Jefferis, David. *Micro Machines: Ultra-Small World of Nano Technology Science Frontiers.* New York, NY: Crabtree Publishing Co., 2006.

Johnson, Rebecca L. *Nanotechnology.* Minneapolis, MN: Lerner Publications, 2006.

Maddox, Dianne. *Nanotechnology.* Farmington Hills, MI: Blackbirch Press, 2005.

Poole, Charles P., and Frank J. Owens. *Introduction to Nanotechnology.* Hoboken, NJ: Wiley, 2003.

Ratner, Mark A. *Nanotechnology: A Gentle Introduction to the Next Big Idea.* Upper Saddle River, NJ: Prentice Hall, 2003.

Scientific American. *Understanding Nanotechnology.* New York, NY: Warner Books, 2002.

# Index